PURE

Modernity, Philosophy, and the One

PURE

MODERNITY, PHILOSOPHY, AND THE ONE

Mark Anderson

⊕

SOPHIA PERENNIS

SAN RAFAEL, CA

First published in the USA
by Sophia Perennis
© Mark Anderson 2009

All rights reserved

Series editor: James R. Wetmore

No part of this book may be reproduced or transmitted,
in any form or by any means, without permission

For information, address:
Sophia Perennis, P.O. Box 151011
San Rafael, CA 94915
sophiaperennis.com

Library of Congress Cataloging-in-Publication Data

Anderson, Mark, 1966–
Pure: modernity, philosophy, and the one / Mark Anderson

p. cm.

ISBN 978 1 59731 094 9 (pbk: alk. paper)
1. Philosophy, Modern. I. Title.
B791.A53 2009
190—dc22   2009018132

CONTENTS

Introduction 1

Happiness and Eudaimonia 5

Reforming the Callicles Inside
  or The Paradox of Self-Habituation 11

American Adolescence 17

Political Decadence 21

Vivisection of Modernity 25

Science and Metaphysics 34

Nietzschean Reflections Contra Nietzsche 43

Experimental Subversions of Modernity 54

Purification 71

Epilogos 107

We *are* something other than scholars: but it is unavoidable that we are also, among other things, scholarly. We have other needs, a different way of growing, a different digestion: we require more, we also require less.

FRIEDRICH NIETZSCHE

INTRODUCTION

This is a book of recovery. It is the story of one man's struggle against the intellectual and existential disorder called Modernity. "Story" is not quite the correct word, for it is not a narrative. It has the content and something of the structure of an intellectual autobiography, but not the form. Perhaps it is a work of philosophy. Yet it most definitely is not Modern philosophy, for all that it is is opposed to the modern. Neither is it Contemporary philosophy, for it contributes nothing to the accumulation of scholarly data.

As philosophy, this little work descends from the reflections of Marcus Aurelius, familiar to us under the title τὰ εἰς ἑαυτόν, which we may loosely translate as *Thoughts to Himself*. It is at once a record of and a reflection upon ἄσκησις. This word, from which comes our word "asceticism," means in this context something like *spiritual discipline*. But this work is more than a report of spiritual discipline undertaken or accomplished. The writing of the text was itself an act of ἄσκησις. Approached with the right intention, one's reading of it can be such an act as well.

The title of the work alludes to a specific type of spiritual discipline known to the Greeks as κάθαρσις. We are familiar with this word in English as "catharsis," but in this text it has a distinctively technical meaning best captured by the word *purification*. The ancients regarded purification as a way of healing, or rather a way of life that is also a healing. For Plato, purification was a charm against a philosophical illness for which he had no name, but which we recognize as Modernity by the symptoms he recorded.

Modernity is not primarily a historical era. It is an assortment of intellectual assumptions, biases, and tendencies to which humans have been susceptible from time immemorial. As a disorder, modernity has profoundly debilitating effects on the person, psychological as well as physiological effects. In extraordinary cases it may spread to social and political institutions, breeding decadence on a vast scale. There were isolated outbreaks of modernity even among the ancients, but it never attained to the level of an epidemic. As a designation of roughly the last five hundred years of Western history, the term modernity denotes an era during which every sector of society has been more or less infected. Today, modernity threatens to become a pandemic.

The typically modern individual suffers from a variety of ailments: melancholy; lethargy; malaise accompanied by a hauntingly vague disorientation; a sense of meaninglessness. In short, nihilism. Many try to escape their dis-ease by diverting attention away from their troubled minds through various bodily indulgences. The most popular of these diversions are of course alcohol and drug abuse, sexual promiscuity, obsessive attachment to popular culture, extreme athletic exertions. Anything that inhibits thought. The typical modern society condones and even promotes these activities, in part because the markets upon which such societies depend profit from the products and services associated with them; also because these societies lack the spiritual resources to recognize them as pernicious.

We can inoculate ourselves against the degenerative effects of modernity by identifying and combating the intellectual assumptions from which the disorder germinates. This procedure involves, according to the treatment prescribed by Platonism, the practice of purification. As a topic of philosophical concern, purification is inseparable from the Platonic tradition, which considers philosophy a way of life leading to deliverance from the bonds of worldly decadence. For the Platonist, the practice of philosophy is itself a purificatory act.

We no longer believe this, for we live and think in obedience to the very *Weltanschauung* that overthrew the Platonic conception

INTRODUCTION

of philosophy. We are moderns; our intellects have been formed by the anti-traditional ideas promulgated by such paradigmatically modern philosophers as René Descartes, David Hume, and Immanuel Kant. But the philosopher whose ideas are most antithetical to the life of purification is Friedrich Nietzsche. Although Nietzsche portrayed himself as a lonely giant mightily opposing the onrush of modernity, his work in fact represents the culmination of the very disorder for which Plato long ago prescribed the regime of κάθαρσις.

There is a sense in which we can understand the intellectual history of the West as a prolonged struggle between Platonism and Nietzscheanism. Recovery from modernity begins with the rejection of Nietzsche, for to reject Nietzsche is to reject the tradition of modernity that produced him. The most effective way to oppose Nietzsche is to participate in the Platonic tradition. Thus, a formula: Platonism is the antidote to modernity.

Philosophers in the Platonic tradition often refer to the vicious soul as disordered or sick. This is more than a literary trope. The image is based on the fact that a soul committed to false assumptions is intellectually incapable of correcting itself. The modern soul is sick in this way. One cannot reason one's way out of modernity, for the illness infects and impairs reason itself. One requires treatment; one requires a cure. This little book is a testament to the possibility of health.[1]

---

1. In all that follows the reader must bear in mind that "modernity" is not a historical designation. This applies also to another term employed throughout this text, "premodern." For our purposes, *Premodernism* is synonymous with *Platonism*. Synonymous with both are designations such as "the ancients." Unless context suggests otherwise, the reader should interpret these terms according to their intellectual, rather than historical, connotations.

Another point: Platonic premodernism as it concerns us in this book is a system of *metaphysics*. All references and allusions to metaphysics should be understood in light of the primary texts of Platonism, in particular the dialogues of Plato and the *Enneads* of Plotinus. Dissociated from the arguments and analyses of these and related texts, metaphysics all too easily degenerates into airy verbiage.

HAPPINESS AND EUDAIMONIA

Ours is a culture obsessed with happiness. Happiness is the standard according to which we measure the worth of our lives. So infatuated are we that we have dedicated our most esteemed cultural resources—the development and manufacture of drugs—to the acquisition and maintenance of happiness. It was not always thus: the infatuation—and its pharmacological corollary—are symptoms of the subjective turn of modernity. Among the Greeks one searches in vain for a word that designates precisely what we mean by "happiness." The premodern world is objectivist; for the ancients the good life amounts to more than the attainment of subjective states like psychological well-being, contentment, bliss. For Plato, as for Aristotle, the good life is a life of eudaimonia, which is an objective phenomenon. Ironically, scholars inevitably translate "eudaimonia" with our word "happiness," which reveals not only the gulf that separates us from the ancients, but our inability to measure—perhaps even to perceive—this expanse. The irony here is that the core of what we moderns mean by "happiness" is *directly opposed* to what the ancients meant by "eudaimonia."

In contemporary usage "happiness" is synonymous with "contentment," "joy," "a good mood;" it is the opposite of "sadness," and like "sadness" it designates a *feeling*, a subjective state of mind. If asked whether we are happy, we have only to introspect and evaluate our emotional or psychological condition. To be sure, we may address the issue by reflecting on more than just our *present* mental state. We may consider whether we are happy *these days*, recently, over some extended period of time; for we might believe that being happy is a relatively stable and lasting condition. Nevertheless, whether we conceptualize happiness as ephemeral or as a more enduring condition, the fact remains that we consider it a subjective state of mind.

Eudaimonia is altogether different. It designates, not a subjective state of mind, but an objective condition of being; it signifies, not how one feels, but how or what one is. "Eudaimonia," in short, means "good life." The "good" here is not a matter of opinion; it is not whatever one believes or feels to be good. It designates what really is good, as a matter of objective fact. This distinction is at the root of the difference between our notion of "happiness" and the Greek idea of "eudaimonia." The good life, eudaimonia, is not whatever someone happens to believe or say that it is, even if that person is passionately committed to his opinion. You may believe deeply that, say, 115 x 23 is 2,650; but it is not (it is 2,645). You may premise physiological research upon the idea that the brain's principal function is to cool the blood; but you would be wrong, however sincerely you believe it and however painful it may be to acknowledge your mistake. Similarly, Plato would say that a man who believes that a life of idleness and self-indulgence is a good life is gravely mistaken.[2]

This is not to deny that a life of self-indulgence is pleasurable. It may be very pleasurable indeed (for a time anyway). But pleasure, like "happiness," is a feeling, or a sensation. The mere fact that a particular activity is pleasurable, that it makes one "happy," is not sufficient to determine that activity as good. Consider the criminal: his pleasure does not make his crimes good. If we inform him that he is living a bad life, he may vehemently disagree; he may insist that his pleasure and his own personal opinion are

---

[2]. If the reader is more inclined to accept the objectivity of math or physiology than of morality, he might consider *why* morality appears different. Is it because we cannot demonstrate the moral claim with a calculator or a scalpel—because it appeals to principles we cannot see, hear, or touch? If this is one's reason, one should ask oneself whether this is a *good* reason.

HAPPINESS AND EUDAIMONIA

decisive. Plato would argue that there is much more at issue. He would not deny that the man derives pleasure from his activities. He would insist that the activities are bad and that the man is living a bad life. He would contend, moreover, that something is wrong with a man who enjoys bad activities. That a man derives pleasure from a bad act not only does not make the act good, it makes the man bad: he who derives pleasure from bad acts is a bad man living a bad life.[3] The good man living a good life derives pleasure from good acts; bad acts, should he perform them, would cause him pain.

Do not mistake this for a rejection of pleasure. The good life is naturally pleasant—pleasure naturally attends, or follows from, the good. But a pleasant life is not necessarily good, for some pleasures are produced by bad acts and are therefore indicative of the opposite of a good life. To put this idea in a formula: Where eudaimonia is, pleasure is as well. Where there is pleasure, eudaimonia may or may not be present.

All of this amounts to an account of moral realism, or objectivism, as opposed to moral subjectivism, or relativism. The objectivist believes that moral terms, terms such as "good," "right," and "just," designate real properties whose status is *independent of* an individual's or a culture's opinions, beliefs, customs, or traditions. The moral relativist believes that morality *depends upon and is conditioned by* an individual's or a culture's beliefs, customs, or traditions. In other words, whatever an individual (or a culture) believes to be good or just *is* good or just for that individual (or for that culture). According to this view, there are no real, independent moral facts.

---

3. He who regularly does bad things is a bad man; he who enjoys doing bad things is even *worse*—he is wicked. That a man enjoys doing what is bad does not prove that what we took to be bad is in fact good. It proves, rather, that the man is perverse.

7

Premodern thinkers such as Plato and Aristotle teach that there *are* moral facts and that humans can know them (which is not to say it is easy to know them; it is not). In the *Gorgias*, for example, Plato situates eudaimonia at the center of Socrates' dispute with Callicles. Callicles identifies eudaimonia with pleasure. Socrates resists this equation, contending that only the self-disciplined man is eudaimôn; the man who devotes his life to unrestrained and undirected hedonism is miserable. Like eudaimonia, "miserable" designates an objective state, not a feeling. Not, "he *feels* miserable," as we might say of someone suffering from the flu; but, "he *is* miserable," as in, "he is wretched" or "he is bad."[4] According to the premodern understanding of eudaimonia—the realist/objectivist understanding—one may say, "He does not *feel* miserable, but he *is* miserable." This is just another way of saying, "He may be happy-as-feeling, but he is not happy-as-eudaimonia."

So if pleasure or subjective feelings do not guarantee eudaimonia, what does? Unfortunately, nothing *guarantees* it. We may act always and only according to what is good, but we never have complete control over our lives. External circumstances intervene; so does fate or chance. King Priam of Troy may very well have loved and lived for the good. But one day the Sons of the Achaeans descended upon his city and destroyed all that he held dear. His life did not end well, however virtuously he may have lived throughout his many years upon this earth. So, to repeat, *nothing* guarantees eudaimonia. Yet we can identify some necessary conditions, conditions without which one is guaranteed *not* to have it. These are the virtues. The standard list of the Classical Greek virtues includes wisdom, justice, temperance, courage, and piety. To "have" these virtues is to act and to feel in particular ways—to act, that is, virtuously, and to feel good at so acting.

---

4. As Socrates puts it in the *Meno*, "What else is being miserable than to desire and to acquire bad things?" (78A 7–8).

HAPPINESS AND EUDAIMONIA

When one acts virtuously, one does what is good. Thus a virtuous life is a life full of good acts; it is, in short, a good life.[5]

This account of virtue illuminates the distinction between happiness-as-feeling and happiness-as-eudaimonia. The virtues are actions—or, more accurately, dispositions toward actions, *habits*. Actions or habits are real, objective conditions of being; they are most definitely not feelings, subjective states of mind (though they do have some bearing on, or relation to, these). Merely feeling oneself to be courageous does not make one so.

Consider our contemporary understanding of happiness. We use the word in such a way that it makes sense to say that an ignorant, cowardly, drug-addled criminal is happy. We might deplore the fact that a bad man can be happy; we might not believe or say that he is. Nevertheless, nothing in our understanding of happiness precludes it. Eudaimonia *does* preclude it. If the virtues are necessary conditions for eudaimonia, then it is not only morally but logically impossible for the vicious man to be eudaimôn. According to premodern usage, then, it *makes no sense* to say that the criminal is eudaimôn.

Plato would say that the vicious man is mistaking pleasure or happiness (in its contemporary sense) for eudaimonia, as Callicles does in the *Gorgias*, and as many of our contemporaries do every day. But this is to confuse a subjective with an objective phenomenon; it is, to say it once more, to confuse a state of mind with a state of being, a feeling with a mind-independent reality.

The ancient Platonists often insist upon a distinction between seeming and being, between that which *appears* to be *x* and that which *really is x*. The distinction takes many forms: it applies to everything from the difference between mere opinion and

---

5. The best ancient account of this—perhaps the best account, period—is in Aristotle's *Nicomachean Ethics*, Books I and II in particular.

knowledge to the difference between the physical and the metaphysical. The distinction between pleasure or "happiness" and eudaimonia falls under this division. Pleasure or "happiness" may *seem* or *appear* to be good. Eudaimonia *really is* good.

REFORMING THE CALLICLES INSIDE
or
THE PARADOX OF SELF-HABITUATION

1

Aristotle says that the intemperate man, the man who desires the bad but believes it to be good, is incurable (*Nicomachean Ethics*, 1150A22). The intemperate man's character and reason are equally corrupt. Mistakenly believing that his bad actions are good, he performs them willingly and with pleasure. Such a man is incurable because there is no right in him to influence and effect change in that which is wrong. Consider, in contrast, the incontinent man, the man who desires that which he knows to be bad. He can change, for his sound reason can override his unsound desires and direct him toward the good. He has developed bad habits, but he has learned enough to know that they are bad. The intemperate man has developed bad habits and has learned nothing, or he has learned the wrong things. He has been thoroughly miseducated. Though he occasionally acts in conformity with the good, he does so only through some variety of external compulsion. The intemperate man will never be virtuous; therefore, he will never be happy (i.e., eudaimôn).

2

The problem: The relentless adolescentization of American culture has produced generations of adults who lack genuine education, education in the Aristotelian sense—education, that is, in virtue, in the proper ordering of our relation to pleasures and pains. It is not that we have learned nothing; rather, we have learned the wrong things. We have been habituated to vice.

This raises the following questions: Can an intemperate adult overcome his miseducation? Can a person with bad habits and false beliefs habituate himself to the good? How can a man who desires base pleasures come to apprehend them as base, experience them as pains, and finally desire noble pleasures? In short, is the intemperate man curable? Can he cure himself?

3

(1) The product of a genuine education is an ordinate soul. The ordinate soul is properly ordered to the hierarchy of being and value: it loves the lovable, desires the good, and admires the beautiful.

Order is produced in the soul through the inculcation of habits that bind our pleasures to that which is good and our pains to that which is bad.

A soul thus habituated is virtuous.

(2) Habits productive of a virtuous soul must be instilled in the young, for our earliest appetites and aversions influence the disposition of our pleasures and pains throughout our lives.

Our appetites and affections, our pleasures and pains, influence in turn the formation of our beliefs, for we readily assent to propositions and ideas that conform to our habits and so please us, whereas we tend to deny that which it pains us to believe.

(3) The traditional agents of education are family, friends, and social, political, and religious institutions.

REFORMING THE CALLICLES INSIDE

Our contemporary educational institutions have been shaped by a tradition that denies the existence of a hierarchy of being and value.

Thus, we have no idea of a properly ordered soul.

Therefore, we do not understand virtue.

Since the aim of genuine education is the production of virtue by ordering the soul to the natural hierarchy of being and value, and since we no longer believe or even understand these things, our contemporary educational institutions inevitably *mis*educate the young.

(4) The miseducated individual has a disordered soul; he is intemperate.

The intemperate man desires that which is bad, which he mistakenly believes to be good.

A soul disordered in this way strives for the satisfaction of base desires.

He who satisfies his base desires, who not only acts badly but is pleased to do so, is deprived of eudaimonia.

The intemperate man, therefore, is miserable.

(5) The only hope for an intemperate man is to realize that his soul is disordered, that his desires are base.

But here we encounter *a problem that is perhaps a paradox*: the intemperate man must come to believe and to feel that the pleasures to which he has become habituated are bad. But the very experience of pleasure draws him toward itself, and thus away from the implications of those experiences or teachings that might lead him to believe that his pleasures are bad and to experience them as pains.

(6) Can the intemperate man, conditioned by false beliefs and base desires, be honest with himself? Can he *know himself*, which in this instance means to admit the disordered state of

his soul? If he can admit this, he can commence the laborious process of reforming his relation to pleasures and pains, of *self*-habituation, *self*-education.

The key and the most difficult act, therefore, is this: to acknowledge that one's desires are base; to say, "I love this, but I ought not to; or I ought to love something else more."

4

In sum: If habits influence our beliefs and desires, and if our habits are bad and we therefore incline toward false beliefs and base desires, how will we learn that our habits are bad; how will we desire to develop good habits, habits associated with true beliefs and noble desires? In short, given an assortment of false beliefs and desires for that which is bad, whence come true beliefs and a desire for the good?

The mind must change fundamentally; the soul must turn. We must come to believe that the object of our desires is bad. But precisely here we meet resistance. Our body desires it, as does some part of our soul. It pleases us. To pronounce it bad is to say that we *should not* desire it, that it *should not* please us. But the very fact that it pleases us makes this almost impossible to say.

5

Contributing factors: Many people in our society have a stake in promoting and maintaining our disordered souls, especially those who obtain money or power from generating and manipulating our unnecessary desires. This explains their constant exertions to persuade us that from our preteen years until well into adulthood it is acceptable to behave in the manner of an immature teenager. The teenager is not yet master of his desires; fads and clever marketing easily seduce him. He has little or no responsibility; he also has a disposable income, which no one prevents him from spending however he chooses. He is a member of a treasured demographic. He is a target.

The teenager is an easy mark, but his financial resources are limited. This latter fact is a natural check on the power and influence of those who manipulate the cultural market to their private advantage. Yet these cunning profiteers have discovered an artificial means to circumvent this obstacle: they promote and enable a cultural environment that facilitates the development of individuals who have the desires of a teenager and the income of an adult—individuals, in short, who desire all that they see and who have the funds to purchase whatever they desire. Hence the mainstreaming of pop-music, video games, pornography, and addiction, all of which appeal to our unnecessary desires and contribute to their boundless expansion.

6

More: Whatever its origins and original intentions, postmodernism has subverted our educational institutions. Postmodernist educators teach their students that the soul (if they admit the term) has no proper order, that there is no hierarchy of being and value to provide a standard against which to evaluate our pleasures and pains. This view is especially appealing to the young, whose souls have yet to be properly formed. It excuses their decadence.

The average university student is egregiously unprepared for a genuinely higher education. He is certainly unprepared in a narrowly academic sense. Worse, his soul has not been cultivated. Students today enter university with a disordered relation to pleasures and pains. Thus, when they are taught that "we live in a postmodern world" and that this implies that no ordering of the soul is better or worse than another, they have an excuse to avoid moral and intellectual maturation, to avoid education.

The postmodern academy impedes genuine education. It is an instrument in the hands of those whose wealth and power depend upon our susceptibility to their machinations. They pull the strings of our desires and we dance to their tune. It is a song of decadence.

Postmodernism, which markets itself as an enemy of ideology in the name of liberation, is in fact a totalitarian ideology of decadence: *liberation of desire is enslavement of the person.*

7

The desire that underlies all others is the desire to do what you like, what you will, what seems good to you (ποιεῖν ὅτι ἂν αὐτοῖς δόξῃ, as Plato puts it in the *Gorgias*). This desire, without knowledge of the good, is the most harmful, and thus also the basest, of desires. It is our decadence.

AMERICAN ADOLESCENCE

1

When we are young and superficial, these things are so much simpler. The objects of our admiration, for example; and what this admiration means, what it demands of us.

2

One has as many masters as one has vices, says Augustine. To adapt this to our environment: one has as many masters as one has liberated unnecessary desires. In Augustine's formulation the masters are the vices themselves. Our masters are those who manipulate our desires for their own power and profit.

3

Our obsession with music is a new phenomenon in human history—like wars of mass destruction and widespread morbid obesity.

4

Dionysian intoxication and adolescent inebriation have nothing in common. The contextualizing intellectual assumptions are fundamentally different. Dionysus is a god, a jealous god who demands that we acknowledge his divinity. Our contemporary revelers reject divinity altogether—unless one counts the decadent deification of their own bodies and physical impulses.

5

That which is "cool" falls on the appearance side of the appearance/reality divide. It designates the external, the superficial, the pose; style, attitude, image. In short, the cool is that which *seems* as opposed to that which *is*. If it is not laudable, it is at least understandable that cool is the aspiration of the young. That it is the aspiration of the mature is a token of the degeneration and decadence of our culture.

6

People who act as if they are always on stage strike us as players in a mediocre production.

7

The need to call attention to oneself is a mark of inferiority. (A psychologist would have written "insecurity.")

8

Image matters *only if* we endeavor to project one. But to cultivate an image in and of itself sullies one's image.

9

A certain type of intellectual admires Nietzsche's maxim that one must give style to one's character—the type that cannot fathom his remark that above all he hates poses.

10

The aging former radical and the present-day adolescent are intellectually indistinguishable. This is an objection to them both.

11

The First Commandment of contemporary America: Thou Shalt Not Mature. Hence blue jeans, video games, popular music, and pot. And how religious our atheists turn out to be!

12

The many products of popular culture rated *M*, for "mature," should of course be rated *I*.

13

The average adolescent insists that he disdains consumerism. He also has a tattoo, piercings, an iPod, and a joint, all of which he desires because of fads. But faddishness is the engine that powers consumerism.

14

Sex, drugs, rock & roll—and shopping. Consumerism is a *natural* adjunct of the pop-culture trinity. Each of these phenomena depends upon and promotes the liberation of unnecessary desires.

15

In the past fifty years the average American teenager has usurped the roles traditionally assigned to the philosopher, sage, and priest. Today we measure the good life by the standards of the infantile fantasies of the American adolescent. More, we employ all the resources of culture (advertising, of course; but politics and education as well) to ensure that no one escapes this mode of evaluation.

16

Self-overcoming: at twenty we hope that when we are forty our attitudes and affect will not have changed. When we are forty we understand that if our adolescent hope had been realized, the intervening years would have been wasted.

17

The problem and the paradox: our beliefs at twenty are influenced more by the misguided teenagers we recently were than by the mature thinkers we may one day become. Our as-yet-nonexistent better selves must reach back in time and wrest us from the influence of our all-too-real past.

18

The young man stays up late hoping that something will happen. The mature man knows that it won't and that it's probably better that way.

19

Youth, in a way, is a state of health. In another way, and in a deeper sense, it is a sickness.

POLITICAL DECADENCE

1

The history of the West is a story of the slow but inexorable liberation and ascendancy of the slavish elements of man. This is the paradigmatic slave revolt. The social upheavals identified by Nietzsche as *Sklavenaufstände* are externalized manifestations of this underlying struggle of our slavish appetites to free themselves from the discipline that constrains them.

2

The rebellion of body against spirit, which becomes self-conscious in Nietzsche, is *our* decadence. The spirit-*weltanschauung* characteristic of Platonism had its foolishnesses, extremes, and casualties; but it served its purpose, namely *self-discipline*. The "liberation of the body" means submission to appetite, which means decadence. The "subjugation of body to reason or spirit" at least meant order; it provided the soil necessary for the growth of genius and various species of greatness.

3

Should we label Foucault's philosophy decadent romanticism or romantic decadence? Perhaps *decadent adolescent romanticism*. Some version of this has become our dominate philosophy.

4

Political decadence: autonomy of the undisciplined individual.

5

There is a time of life when the neglect of politics is a sign of intellectual immaturity. There is a later time when to concern oneself with politics is a mark of this same vice. When one is young, one neglects the political in favor of superficial ephemera. With intellectual maturity one realizes that, compared to *ta metaphysika*, politics itself is superficial and ephemeral. The permanent things, the "accursed questions," take precedence.

6

Journalists regard the waning of their influence as evidence of our culture's intellectual decline. Serious intellectuals regard journalism itself as evidence of cultural decline.

7

The exploitation of democracy by unchecked capitalism is a natural and inevitable phenomenon. Democracy in its essence is bound up with Utilitarianism on the one hand and Nihilistic Hedonism on the other—and perhaps in the end these are not two different hands.

8

Ancient modernity: democracy is an option wherever body rebels against the authority of soul. But this means that democracy is premised upon the rejection of metaphysics, and hence upon the disintegration of tradition. The phenomenon of Athenian democracy teaches that even among the ancients tradition was in decline and the modern was stirring.

9

The initial stages of decadence smell sweet—hence Classical Athens and Renaissance Florence.

10

If only the material realm exists, then democracy may well be the ideal form of government. If there is something more, something ontologically prior, government should be in the hands of an *acknowledged elite*—some version of a theocracy (though in this case *god* need not mean God).

11

The Reactionary: Not the size of government, but the end and aim of government is the salient matter. The ancients teach that the object of the political art is the production of virtuous citizens. In this they go further than America's founders. John Adams knew that the well-being of our society and our government depends upon the virtue of the citizenry. Plato knew more: he taught that the virtue of the citizenry depends upon the government's inculcation and promotion of specific habits and social institutions.

No man can become good, and no good man can flourish, in a decadent and corrupt culture. Therefore, governmental authority must extend even into those cultural concerns that we moderns are accustomed to regard as inviolably private.

12

No, do not Question Authority. Question Power. If you cannot tell the difference, ask an authority. He will know.

13

In American politics one encounters a fountain of youth, for democracy makes children of us all.

14

"Dissent is the highest form of patriotism." This may be true *in a democracy*. But does this indicate something noble in dissent or something ignoble in democracy?

15

The democrat is the man who mistakes the freedom to choose the good for choosing the good freely.

16

Human happiness consists in contemplation of the divine.
Politics is a distraction from the divine—it drags one *down*.
Democracy draws everyone into politics, and thus away from the source and cause of human happiness.
Is democracy, then, *misanthropic?*

VIVISECTION OF MODERNITY

1

To identify the characteristic intellectual patterns of modernity and the assumptions that support them, and to expose the first principles beneath these. To find one's way out of the labyrinth of these principles. Not to reject them, but to ignore them; to forget them. The premodern does not reject the modern, it simply does not know it; it lives without the modern.

To argue with Hume, for example, is to concede the victory to modernity. We must not refute Hume, we must refuse to converse with him—we must forget him.

2

Modernity: reductivist methodology; empiricist epistemology; materialist ontology; mechanistic physics; hedonistic ethics; radical politics.

3

Modernity in one word: *subjectivism*. This explains the substitution of relativism for realism; epistemology for ontology; happiness for eudaimonia; personality for soul; bliss for the divine.

4

That bliss you are following leads in one direction only—to the bottom of the well of modernity.

5

Freud attributes man's discontent to the supposed fact that civilization frustrates our search for happiness, which he identifies with pleasure. The Platonist knows that only *modern* man is discontented in this way, and that the source of his trouble is this impoverished view of happiness.

6

Modern melancholia, though productive of a certain type of art, undermines one's health. The melancholy artist might approach the profound, but he will never attain the sublime.

7

To repeat the shibboleth, "Beauty is in the eye of the beholder," is to say, "I, too, am a modern." The premodern man says, "Beauty is in the eye of the beautiful." He knows that ugly eyes—undisciplined, uneducated, vicious eyes—are blind.

8

A healthy body contributes to a sound mind. But a virtuous soul is necessary for the production and maintenance of a healthy body. Hence, *pace* Nietzsche, Plato is correct: Soul is fundamental.

9

We presume that Plotinus' encounter with the One had its subjective correlative, its phenomenological aspect. His was what we might call a "mystical experience." On the other hand, if we take "to become one with the divine" in its strictest sense, then perhaps such a thorough identification with the One, resulting in a radical

VIVISECTION OF MODERNITY

de-identification and separation from the physical, will leave no trace on the conscious mind. Plotinus himself wrote that the soul when unified cannot distinguish itself from the One and so can neither recognize nor relate the event. Unification gives rise, not to knowledge, but to a presence beyond knowing (6.9.3–4).

Plotinus evinced no interest in trying to describe his experience (nor did Porphyry after his vision; nor Aquinas later). In any case, whether or not unification has a phenomenological correlate, the subjective aspect is secondary, derivative, beside the point. This is the *premodern* attitude. For modern man the subjective *experience* is everything. For the premodern the *object* of the experience is all that really matters.

10

Modernity's inward turn is not in itself objectionable, for the One dwells within. But modern man seeks only himself inside, his so-called consciousness, his so-called self. What he calls his "true self" emphasizes *self*. The Platonist turns inward to find a way out; he seeks his true self with an emphasis on *true*.

In the One, which is the proper goal of the inner search, the Platonist finds, not the modern self, but rather the source of whatever may legitimately be called the self, which is in fact the source of all, the ἀρχή, τὸ θεῖον, τὸ ἕν.

11

The modern self is a fiction. Even the skeptical Hume was gullible on this point, which is why his failure to locate the self so dismayed him. The anxiety and despair of the Existentialists resulted in part from their mistaken beliefs about the self. Nietzsche knew the remedy for our affliction: we must abandon

27

the self as a fabrication of modern philosophy. This one act will not only cure us of Existential melancholy; it will eradicate the plague inflicted upon us by the Existentialists' cousins the psychoanalysts, namely the conviction that our selves can be fragmented, fractured, cracked, and broken.

12

The conception of modernity as subjectivism accounts for its philosophical beginnings in Descartes as well as for more recent movements and tendencies of thought—Existentialism, for example. But whereas Descartes intentionally employed subjectivism to what he believed to be his methodological advantage, the Existentialists inherited it as a given and suffered from it.

13

Heidegger everywhere holds out the promise of a return to Being, but his road back to the Presocratics is only a detour on his way to Existentialism.

14

Postmodernism does not represent the overcoming of modernity, but rather the development of modernity's premises to their logical conclusion. It is parasitic upon modernity, and must therefore always be qualified with quotation marks, thus: "Post"-modern.

15

If postmodernism accomplishes anything, it reveals the contradictions at the heart of modernity. This should lead to the abandonment of these premises, and immediately thereafter to the dissolution of the postmodern, which is founded upon them. The survival of postmodernism indicates that its practitioners and adherents mistake the premises of modernity for the first principles of reality, which not only contradicts their professed philosophical commitments, but exposes their dependence upon modernity's intellectual assumptions. The "Post" has always been a lie.

16

One employs irony to distance oneself from others. Rorty enjoins us to be ironic toward ourselves and our own beliefs. His brand of irony, therefore, distances one from oneself, which is to say it produces a psychological breach. But this is a type of mental disorder.

Here we have a purely modern phenomenon: only in modernity is the self regarded as an entity of the sort that can be fractured—and only a decadent modern would encourage us to fracture it.

17

It is not Pragmatism to reject a philosophy—Pragmatism itself, for example—on the grounds that it inevitably destroys the individual or civilization that accepts it. The objection is not limited to the claim that the philosophy is destructive, which may very well be a merely Pragmatic argument. The objection is rather that the fatality of the philosophy provides evidence of its falsehood. This is an appeal to the relevance and the power of truth, which certainly is not Pragmatism.

18

One may appeal to the assumptions of historicism to explain the genesis of a false proposition; but an idea's historical contingency cannot by itself determine it as false. In other words, the claim that "all ideas, all philosophies, are historically contingent and therefore false" is false. So what are the historical conditions that produce this claim?

19

The phrase "House of Atreus" connotes the ancestors as well as the descendents of Atreus, Tantalus as well as Orestes. Just so does "Platonism" embrace everyone from Pythagoras to Plotinus.

20

Of Longinus Plotinus said, "He is a scholar, but he is not at all a philosopher." We might say the same of those intellectual historians who insist upon distinguishing Platonism from Neoplatonism. Plotinus, the supposed founder of "Neoplatonism," knew nothing of this distinction; he considered himself a loyal Platonist. He may have elaborated Plato's central themes; no doubt he illuminated what was only dimly implicit in the master's written works; but he consistently maintained that he derived his ideas from the tradition that descended from Plato. He was taken at his word for nearly two thousand years.

Then came historicism.

In the nineteenth century, certain German scholars claiming to have detected previously unperceived fissures separating Plotinus' ideas from pure Platonism, declared Plotinus the unwitting founder of a new school of thought, inspired by but diverging from Platonism sufficiently to merit the prefix "Neo." Thus died a tradition that had sustained the greatest of Western minds, from Plotinus himself to Michelangelo. It was not a natural death. Platonism as a unified, living, inspirational tradition was assassinated by pedantry, drowned in an inkwell.

VIVISECTION OF MODERNITY

The "decline and fall of the Neoplatonic interpretation of Plato" is a tale of the ascendancy of the modern, historicist, pedantic interpretation of Plato. It represents, to employ Nietzsche's terms, the substitution of a critical for a monumental reading of the history of philosophy.

The inferences one draws from this event depend upon whether one aspires to be a scholar or a philosopher. From the perspective of the intellectual historian, the segregating of Plato from Plotinus is fecund, endlessly productive of the most minute research projects. The philosopher seeks a different sort of fecundity.

The labor of identifying and categorizing the varieties of Platonism and Neoplatonism—in a word, taxonomy—satisfies the instincts of the scholar. The unity of Platonism nourishes the spirits of those who love wisdom. If you long for what counts today as historical accuracy, accept the scholar's distinction between Platonism and Neoplatonism. If you long for wisdom, live the unity of Platonism.

21

The scholar is a skeptic with respect to wisdom: he does not believe in the search; he believes only in research.

22

The manuscript tradition has failed to preserve those sections of the *Nicomachean Ethics* in which Aristotle identifies as virtues the habits characteristic of the modern university research scholar.

23

There is much to be said for knowing what serious scholars have written about Plato. There is infinitely more to be said for knowing what Plato wrote for himself. The trick is to find the mean. But from the mean between *much* and *infinite* the much appears infinitesimal.

24

Contemporary philosophers refuse to admit that Plato meant what he wrote, for what he wrote generally amounts to a repudiation of their moral and intellectual lives.

25

We moderns are suspicious of metaphysical systems, which we have learned to regard as the ideological masks worn by systems of power. Only we, from whose eyes Nietzsche and Foucault have lifted the darkening folds of delusion, see the real motives behind the movements of history. We have access to historical truths to which the historical actors themselves were blind. We know that "God" means "oppressor;" that religious wars are fought for control over material resources; that metaphysical disputes are contests for worldly dominion.

Or do we?

Do our unmaskings demonstrate the scope and penetration of our intellectual vision? Or do they rather expose the impoverishment of our imagination? Actions motivated by that which cannot be measured by the standards of quantity make no sense to us. To comprehend an action we must trace it back to a motive expressible in the vocabulary of matter. If we fail to identify such a motive, we must either fabricate one or pronounce the act inexplicable. This is so because we are materialists; we have no eye for quality except as an attribute supervening on quantity.

Why are we materialists? We do not know; we cannot say; it just seems so obvious to us. But should not our ignorance on this point lead us to suspect that materialism is *our* ideology? It should—and it should motivate us to wonder who benefits from our wearing this mask.

26

Modernity is hubris; decadence is its Nemesis.

SCIENCE AND METAPHYSICS

1

By God, we mean gods.
By gods, we mean the Olympians.
By the Olympians, we mean nature.
By nature, we mean the inscrutable forces of nature.
By the inscrutable forces of nature, we mean the metaphysical reality that manifests itself in and through them; their source; the One.
By the One, we mean God…

2

In nature we see the divine intelligibles (τὰ θεῖα νοητά) expressed as purely as matter—the principle of imperfection—permits.

3

Some thoughts we can no longer think. Plato's Good beyond Being, for example; Nietzsche's Eternal Return. We are no longer *permitted* to entertain such notions, and we have become all but *incapable* of doing so. Ideas unsupported by scholarly research or by the latest pronouncements of the physical sciences have no place in contemporary intellectual life. The footnote pedant and the myopic scientist provide our models of academic respectability. But this means, at a minimum, that we cannot understand the greatest of past philosophers; at worst it means that no great philosopher will arise again in our future.

SCIENCE AND METAPHYSICS

4

The history of the philosophy of science in the twentieth century is a tale of the steady retreat from the naive assumptions of positivist verificationism. But this means a retreat from the position that scientific theories can be known to be true—and, for some, from the position that they can *be* true.

Karl Popper believed that by adhering to his methodology of falsificationism we can at least identify false theories, and he hoped that this procedure might in some way indicate which theories are closer to the truth than others. Theories that survive repeated attempts to falsify them possess "verisimilitude," or so Popper was pleased to imagine. Unfortunately, we have no way to determine whether a theory survives because it is true or because of our own inability to devise the appropriate tests. Therefore, we can make no inference from a theory's survival to its verisimilitude.

More problematic for Popper's proposal, however, is Pierre Duhem's argument that a theory can never finally be falsified because we can always redirect the gravamen of the supposed falsification to some peripheral part of the theory, or to some other set of assumptions in the background of the overall experimental situation.

Paul Feyerabend extended and radicalized the assault on these attempts to identify the distinguishing characteristics of a scientific theory and to justify the assumed authority of science as the arbiter of truth. He insisted that every successful scientific theory has at some time been falsified, and that no account of science based on either verificationism or falsificationism can possibly be accurate because there simply is no "scientific method."

Then there is Thomas Kuhn, the correct formulation of the conclusions of whose work is still controversial, but who demonstrated at least that there is no simple one-to-one representational relationship between even the most successful scientific theory and the external world.

Exhausted, perhaps, from decades of failed attempts to justify our confidence in the veracity of successful scientific theories, philosophers such as Imre Lakatos argue that we must abandon the theory as the object of evaluation. We must focus instead on research programs, about which the best that we can say is that they are fecund.

The old confidence that science discovers the truth about our world is gone, replaced by one or another version of pragmatism or instrumentalism. A scientific theory—or, rather, some appropriately related collection of theories that can be said to constitute a research program—may be useful for some specifiable end. But can we say that it describes reality as it is? Must we accept its ontological apparatus? Quine abandoned these aspirations long ago when he opined that to be is to be the value of a variable. In other words, we can know what entities are postulated by a given theory, and perhaps whether in postulating them the theory is successful ("perhaps," because there is another problem, or set of problems, relating to how we determine which theories are useful or successful); but we cannot legitimately infer from the presence of an entity—an electron, say—in a useful theory that the entity is present in reality.

This pragmatic/instrumentalist account of scientific truth appealed to philosophers like Richard Rorty, who, from the fates of epistemology and the philosophy of science in the twentieth century, concluded that science has no more legitimate claim to truth than does literature. Rorty had his philosophical rivals, and one notes a steady increase in the number and vociferousness of the objections lodged against his brand of neopragmatism, especially as applied to science. Still, it is hard not to believe that, given the assumptions of modernity, some version of the rejection of objectivism or realism necessarily follows.

Einstein's overthrow of Newtonian physics was an early signal that even the most successful theory may very well be false. The event served as a wedge between successful science and truth. But if science cannot boast of possessing the truth, neither can it issue pronouncements concerning the truth status of metaphysics or religion. The conclusions of theoretical physics, for example, have no bearing whatever on such vexing questions as whether or not god or the soul exists. In the first place, since neither god nor the soul is a physical entity, physics, which is necessarily limited to the physical, is incapable of learning anything about them. In the second place, and more importantly, physics' indeterminate truth status renders it impotent to provide a standard against which to evaluate the propositions of metaphysics.

5

Contemporary theoretical physics is so far from being subject to empirical verification that the discipline satisfies Hume's definition of metaphysics. Shall we follow his advice and consign our books on relativity, quantum mechanics, black holes, and dark matter to the flames?

6

Being and Logos: A particle of matter *is* because of an act of existence for which it itself is not responsible. It *is what it is* because of its microstructure, the specific and stable organization of its constitutive elements—in a word, its form, which it itself does not produce. The same is true, *mutatis mutandis*, of forces and laws of nature, which neither bring themselves into being nor cause their specific and essential character.

The materialist would like to explain the world in full by means of the attributes and arrangements of material particles in conjunction with natural forces and the laws that determine their appearance and application. But any such explanation necessarily presupposes the existence and ordered constitution of the particles, the forces, and the laws themselves. Matter and its properties, natural forces and the laws that govern them, are neither self-generating nor self-explanatory; they depend utterly upon the ontologically prior acts of existence and form. Without these metaphysical principles there can be no physical reality.

Moral: physics, being derivative, will never provide the fundamental explanation of reality.

7

There was time when of necessity the philosopher stood with the scientist against the theologian. Today, the alliances have shifted. It is no longer the philosopher's business to defend science against religion, but rather to defend philosophy against scientism.

8

The scientist *should* attack fundamentalism. The metaphysician *should* attack scientism. In this way the scientist purifies religion and the metaphysician purifies the search for knowledge.

9

The natural sciences can neither confirm nor disconfirm a philosopher's metaphysical insights. This is so because *beings* differ from, and are lesser than, *Being*. Physics and metaphysics address distinct levels of the ontological hierarchy.

10

Science and religion cannot conflict, not because the former deals with facts and the latter with values. They both deal with facts *and* values—the "distinction between 'is' and 'ought'" is the illegitimate product of a typical modern misunderstanding (and Gould's fantasy of "Non-Overlapping Magisteria" is just one of many naive manifestations of this supposed distinction). The relevant difference is that science refers to physical reality while religion refers to the metaphysical.

Fundamentalism and scientism misunderstand this distinction. They force a conflict by reducing reality to a single ontological plane—the physical—at which point each insists that its own statements about reality thus misconceived are correct. But only science properly refers to the physical, which is why fundamentalism inevitably comes off badly in the dispute.

Fundamentalism misunderstands metaphysical propositions as physical pronouncements, and in doing so it both distorts religion and provides the appearance of respectability to scientism. What is really at issue between science and religion is not the correct understanding of physical phenomena, but whether the physical is the only, or the highest, form of existence.

11

Faith and reason are opposed only within the perspective that produced them; as creatures of this perspective, they are one. They are quarrelling twins born of a daimôn called Modernity. In a traditional mode of thought neither faith nor reason as we moderns conceive of them exists. For the traditionalist, the metaphysical is an object of intuitive knowledge. As intuitive, it is not "rational;" as knowledge, it is not a matter of "faith."

12

Our vision of a chair depends upon neurological activity. A neurologist can cause a patient to experience this and other visions simply by manipulating his brain—by introducing the appropriate drug, for example, or by manually stimulating the relevant neural pathways. This does not persuade us that there really are no chairs, that our visions of chairs are *nothing more than* the electrical-chemical activity inside our skulls. Why then should we believe that artificially induced religious experiences or "the God center" in our brain implies the non-existence of the object of mystical experience?

13

"But no one has formulated a successful argument for God's existence." Is this true? Could it be that we moderns are incapable of understanding the argument? I do not cite my inability to comprehend advanced mathematical proofs as evidence that mathematics is solely a matter of faith.

14

We are inclined to believe in the empirical and to doubt the metaphysical because only the former is supported by "evidence" and "proof." But our standards of evidence and proof have been determined by the canons of empiricism. We inevitably beg the question against metaphysics.

15

No one simply ceases to believe in metaphysics. One *begins* to believe in *something else*—materialism, for example. But the typical materialist concentrates so fixedly upon disproving metaphysics that he neglects to consider whether materialism itself either has been or can be proved.

16

The agnostic neither prays every other day nor attends church twice a month. He lives, thinks, and believes more like an atheist than a theist. Does this demonstrate the impossibility of a sincere agnosticism?

17

The practice of asceticism and the ingestion of hallucinogens both alter our neurochemistry. But one accomplishes this through spiritual discipline, the other through bodily indulgence. The end may be quantitatively identical, but the means are qualitatively distinct. This makes all the difference.

18

Asceticism disciplines the body; through it one ascends to The Vision. The undisciplined indulgence of the body is aestheticism, through which one descends into visions.

19

Find the truth and you will have the vision. Seek the vision and you will find neither.

20

When discussing philosophy, many people speak of truth and knowledge as if they were to say to a scientist, "A black hole for me is a singularity of light and happiness." They do not realize that serious people over the course of millennia have refined our understanding of philosophical concepts and generated thoughtful agreements concerning their meaning and implications (though there are indeed thoughtful dissenters). The proposition, "There is no difference between the truth and a belief about what is true," which is implied by the modern relativist expression "true for me," is a product of ignorance of the discipline of philosophy. We do not countenance such solecisms in science, nor should we when the conversation turns to philosophy.

21

Our objection to modern science is not that it is false (though in many cases it is, at best, unverifiable), but that it obstructs our progress toward truer and more noble destinations of thought.

NIETZSCHEAN REFLECTIONS CONTRA NIETZSCHE

1

Nietzsche's most egregious failing as a philosopher, as a thinker, as a man, is his treatment of Plato. Before Plato Nietzsche lost his nerve. He behaves toward Plato like the dishonest, underhanded caviler and sniper that in all other contexts he disdains. Nietzsche assailed God more directly than he dared to confront Plato. Was he, as a man in his forties, so fat on the adolescent stew of *ressentiment* and recklessness as to pronounce Plato boring? Then this just illustrates his helpless vexation at having to confront a genius more towering than his own. Plato is the original and the supreme philosopher-artist and world historical legislator; he is, in short, the perfect example of a type to which Nietzsche aspired.

Nietzsche never completely acknowledged Plato's role as artist, whether out of peevishness or blindness we cannot say. The man who assiduously practiced the art of reading behind an author's words read Plato's dialogues as if they were so many instruction manuals. He took everything Plato wrote literally; or he pretended to. Why did he read Plato this way? Or, to ask a Nietzschean question, why was it necessary that he read Plato in this way? What drive was exercising its will to power in this instance?

Nietzsche disliked Plato because he suspected, and feared, the truth about himself. Nietzsche was sick, decadent—he at least had the honesty to admit this. He was *fundamentally* unhealthy—about this he dissembled. Plato—the man, the artist, and the universe he created in and through his art—overflows with health, life, exuberance, beauty. The Platonic corpus is a flower of art larger, brighter, more varied, and more sublime than nearly all the other blooms in the art-garden of the West. The Platonic ideal represents a healthfulness and a height from which Nietzsche, decadent and fuming, appears sickly, small, and weak. Nietzsche denounced Plato, *had* to denounce Plato, because he could not equal him. He convinced himself that Plato was hostile to life so that he, Plato's philosophical and physiological opposite, might imagine that he stood with life.

Nietzsche suffered from the same ironical disorder that he diagnosed in so many others: he hoped to will himself into health by masking his decadence with grand illusions.

2

Nietzsche suffered from man, from *modern* man. The false story he told himself about the ancients, and in particular about Socrates and Plato, inoculated him against suffering from *himself*. Nietzsche redefined sickness and called it Platonism to avoid diagnosing his own disease.

3

Nietzsche, not Socrates or Plato, was obsessed with "the value of existence." Was *he*, then, the "moral monster"? He was certainly more—sick.

4

Nietzsche begins "The Problem of Socrates" (*Twilight of the Idols*) by condemning those who pass judgment on life. He ends the chapter by claiming that Socrates did just that, citing as evidence the philosopher's final words, which he interprets to imply that Socrates was eager to die. But this interpretation, for which

Nietzsche provides no justification, merely *illustrates* his assumption that Socrates was hostile to life; it does not *prove* it.

For our part, we see no evidence that Socrates condemned life. To the contrary, he seems rather to have lived life fully and exuberantly, even in its most dangerous aspects. That Socrates sought eudaimonia (which, *pace* Nietzsche, is something other than utilitarian happiness) does not mean that he denied the tragic.

5

Nietzsche associates metaphysical thinking with the degeneration of man, with spiritual weakness and maudlin egalitarianism. But what, specifically, has he to say against a Platonic ethics and political philosophy? He can say nothing, for Plato's is a noble philosophy: he does not teach pity, neighbor love, the virtue of suffering. Plato exhibits none of the sentimentality that Nietzsche insists must attend belief in the beyond.

6

In *The Birth of Tragedy* Nietzsche condemns what he calls Socrates' scientific-Alexandrian spirit. In *The Antichrist* he celebrates science and Alexandrian philology, yet he condemns Socrates once again. In the former work he portrays Socrates as the enemy of myth, which he interprets according to Schopenhauerian metaphysics. But this ignores the mythic and metaphysical elements in Socrates' life and thought. In the latter work he casts Socrates as the enemy of instinct, authority, and aristocracy. This ignores Socrates' political philosophy, as well as his life among the Athenian military class of *kalokagathoi*.

7

Contrary to Nietzsche's repeated assertions, Socrates was not the

PURE: Modernity, Philosophy, and the One

wellspring and paragon of calculative reason. He was not the conquering hero of rationalism, through whom the mob revolted. We must award this title to another—Protagoras, perhaps; or Gorgias. Socrates stood with an altogether different class of men. He stood with the traditionalists, which is to say with the conservative hoplites.

The Sophists unleashed relativism and liberal democracy on Greece. They accomplished this by manipulating speech in such a way as to oblige men to justify their social and political commitments *rationally*. Those with the resources to study with the Sophists learned how to take advantage of this novel situation. They *debated* their way into power. In this way many rich upstarts—men who lacked integrity, dignity, and natural nobility—snatched power away from the honorable old families.

Socrates confronted the Sophists (and the political decadence that afflicted Athens under their influence) on their own terms, which prescribed that he counter them with logoi. Rational argumentation was forced on him by the Sophists' formulation of the debate. He employed it to argue in defense of tradition, *kalokagathia*, and the *patrios politeia*.

8

The tradition that produces democracy and modernity—the decadence of these things—is the Sophistic tradition, *not* the Socratic-Platonic tradition.

9

According to Nietzsche's version of Western intellectual history, philosophy as developed by Socrates and Plato delivered the killing thrust to what he variously classifies as the Homeric or the Tragic mentality. As he tells the story, Platonism, particularly through its influence on Christianity, is responsible for the demise of an authentically ancient worldview and the rise of a decadent modernity. The task he set for himself was to oppose modernity by rejecting effete optimism in favor of the pessimism of strength.

But Nietzsche's reading of history is a tangle of confusions. The Homeric mentality differs from the Tragic, not least in the degree and type of "pessimism" articulated by each. Plato never denied the fragility and ultimate inexplicability of human existence in the manner suggested by Nietzsche's caricature. Plato's late works in particular are never naively optimistic. But more to the point: measured according to the standards of modernity, the Homeric, Tragic, and Platonic mentalities are *one* (which is not to say that they derive from all and only the same fundamental assumptions). Modernity rejects the ancient view altogether, whether it be Homeric, Tragic, Socratic, Platonic, or Christian.

Moreover, Nietzsche's philosophy does *not* overcome modernity. It is a symptom of modernity; it is modern philosophy drawing its logical conclusions. To read Nietzsche is to witness modernity's attempted suicide.

Nietzsche would like to station himself beside Homer in opposition to Plato, but history will not bend this way. The actual conflict is between Homeric-Platonic antiquity and Nietzschean modernity.

10

Socrates fought as a heavily armed infantry soldier on the hot and dusty plains of Greece, blood and sweat spattered on his helmet, hands, and spear. Nietzsche fell from his horse and cracked his sternum.

11

Nietzsche's self-proclaimed intellectual descendents, the Existentialists, failed to discover a philosophical therapy for what ailed them. We modern melancholiacs fail in precisely the same way, and for the same reasons. The intellectual assumptions of modernity distort our understanding of human nature, which prevents us from discovering the cure for our disorder. More, our immersion in modernity causes us even to misdiagnose our affliction.

This problem of misdiagnosis begins—or anyway first appears in grand terms—with Nietzsche himself. His equation of Platonism with sickness, and of his own philosophy with the great health, is a magnificent irony. Nietzsche was sickly and weak. Therefore, judged according to his own standards, his philosophy is unhealthy, which in Nietzschean terms means *false*. But apart from this irony, which amounts in the end to a merely Nietzschean objection, Nietzsche's intellectual assumptions, and thus also the conclusions he derived from them, are too modern to be sound.

Nietzsche went wrong in the same way the Existentialists went wrong; the same way the Postmodernists go wrong today (though, to his credit, Nietzsche would sniff at being associated with the Postmodernists); namely, he formulated his objections to modernity in a thoroughly modern vocabulary. One cannot overthrow modernity from within the modern paradigm. One can play havoc with the system; one can damage, destabilize, and subvert it. But any attempt to destroy it from the inside must fail. It is precisely by devouring itself that the ouroboros survives. Modernity, too, will survive this type of assault, though in a state of disarray and degeneration—a state, that is, of decadence, whether of the Nietzschean, the Existentialist, or the Postmodernist variety.

NIETZSCHEAN REFLECTIONS

Nietzsche attempted to find his way out of modernity by looking to the ancients as a counter-ideal. In this he was only moderately successful, for although he was historicist enough to see the vast intellectual and cultural chasm separating him from the Greeks, he was too burdened by the weight of modernity to overleap the divide.

Nietzsche's one sustained attempt to return to the Greeks—in *The Birth of Tragedy*—is founded upon, and thus conditioned by, Schopenhauer's version of Transcendental Idealism, which descends from Kant's brand of modern philosophy. It does not succeed in overcoming modernity because it is itself a product of modern intellectual assumptions.

Looking back on *The Birth of Tragedy* more than a decade after its original publication, Nietzsche was disappointed and critical. But the "self-criticism" he appended to this work of his youth was still entangled in modernity. In it, Nietzsche continued to ground his opposition to modernity upon modernity's underlying principles. His critique appears radical only because he developed relentlessly the implications of his original premises, not because he rejected the premises themselves.

This deeper rejection, or perhaps "neglect" is the appropriate word, must be the starting point of genuine *pre*modernism, which is the only sure way out of the modern predicament.

12

The profound consists in searching out, revealing, and audaciously dissecting the presuppositions of a system of thought. The sublime consists in the naive (in Schiller's sense of this word) development of noble presuppositions in the direction of their highest potentialities.

PURE: Modernity, Philosophy, and the One

The profound is revolutionary, dangerous. It is, therefore, the aspiration of the young. The sublime, which is related to but in a sense towers over the beautiful, is the preserve of the mature.

Nietzsche is profound. The *Iliad* is sublime.

13

Nietzsche's image of the philosopher was decisively influenced by the Romantics' image of the artist: the pose of alienation, isolation. At bottom, Nietzsche is always Romantic. He is Romantic even in his Positivism, even in his admiration of Thucydidean Realism.

14

The Romanticism of Nietzsche's Classicism distinguishes him from Goethe, who had the strength and good sense to outgrow youth before growing old.

15

Nietzsche believed that "better consciousness" equals "anti-nature." This way of thinking leads to—*amounts to*—decadence.

16

Scratch a depressive and you will expose a Nietzschean who misunderstands Nietzsche—or who understands him all too well.

17

A few strong souls may indeed live nobly as nihilists or radical skeptics. *Hoi polloi* cannot. To publicize, celebrate, and advocate that skepticism, as Nietzsche does, is to provide the mob man with a rationale for his lack of self-discipline, his enslavement to his baser self, his decadence. Was Plato appropriated by the Christians? Nietzsche has been appropriated by degenerates.

18

It is *still* true that our highest impulses are decadent. Yet no "philosophy of the future" has sprung up to counteract the decadence. Postmodernism is not that philosophy: faced with a Derrida or Foucault, Nietzsche would see just one more decadent.

19

Nietzsche first encountered the *problem of the value of truth* during the so-called middle period of his intellectual development. In his revolt against Wagner, against the Wagnerian in himself, he experimented with, and ultimately adopted, the philosophical assumptions of "Enlightenment." For a time he settled—rather uncomfortably as it turned out—into the doctrines of positivism, according to which science is the arbiter of truth. Equating the natural sciences with what he called "historical philosophy," Nietzsche insisted that careful study of the evolution of human thought reveals that the postulate of *being* is an error, that all is *becoming*, and that metaphysics is premised upon all too human misunderstandings.

This is all very strange, for we know that historical research can neither verify nor falsify metaphysical propositions—and this is true even of history as historical philosophy. But historical philosophy (mis)informed by the presuppositions of a materialist scientism can lead one to draw any number of facile conclusions. This is what happened to Nietzsche. He formulated his early analyses of the history of metaphysics in as unreflective a mood as that which possesses the adolescent who has discovered with naive amazement the power of scientific thought. Nietzsche became in his thirties the nihilist we precocious Nietzscheans become today in our teens.

Yet Nietzsche was no mere callow adolescent. With penetrating foresight he divined the social, political, and existential implications of the positivist ideal. He understood that the Enlightenment conception of truth and knowledge—which is a thoroughly *modern* conception (this he did not quite understand)—poses a threat to human health, vitality, and vigor—a threat to individuals and to cultures as well. Science tends to act as a solvent; when applied to weak or unstable bodies its degenerative powers operate with ruthless inexorability.

This line of reasoning led Nietzsche to wonder whether truth is hostile to life. He inclined to believe that it is, and he retained this belief even later in life, long after he had abandoned his unreflective ardor for positivism. In his late works he continues to maintain that human survival depends upon falsehood, that what we call "truth" is an error without which we cannot live.

As a response to this problem of the value of truth Nietzsche proposed a radical affirmation. The noble individual must cheerfully accept the discomfiting fact that untruth is a condition of life. (This very acceptance provides proof of nobility.) Tomorrow's free-spirits and the philosophers of the future will survey mankind's long history of error with no feelings of gloom or despair; they will celebrate the dissolution of all that once passed for Truth; they will be sufficiently light—light of foot and of mind— to dance over the abyss of nihilism.

This way of thinking led Nietzsche to Zarathustra and to his conception of the *Übermensch*. But this will not do for us anti-Nietzscheans, for those of us attempting to shake off the burden of our Nietzschean birthright. We doubt whether Nietzsche's is the only solution to the problem of the value of truth, whether it is the best solution. We suspect that our remedy requires, not that we solve the problem as Nietzsche formulated it, but that we recognize the error of the "problem" itself.

Could it be that *truth* is not the matter, but rather the *modern conception of truth*? If we suppose that truth is hostile to life, then we have at least two options: we may fundamentally alter our approach to life or we may interrogate our understanding (our *modern* understanding) of truth.

We have analyzed the modern conception of truth. We have weighed it in our scales and found it to be lighter than air, lighter than a dream of air. We conclude, therefore, that Nietzsche derived his "problem of the value of truth" from a basic misunderstanding. What must we say, then, of his solution? What *can* one say of a radical procedure devised to treat a fabricated condition? Might it not induce its own debilitating symptoms? Precisely this is the danger of nihilism, even of nihilistic affirmation—as medicine it is a *pharmakon* indeed, for it may very well be poison.

20

Nietzsche boasted of being the world's first perfect nihilist, but also of having *pushed through* nihilism. But this is impossible, for nihilism presents nothing against which to apply pressure. The proper response to nihilism is to turn away and walk back down the road that leads to it, at the entrance to which stand the gates of modernity. There is no need to topple these gates; one need only walk past them, back into the *pre*modern.

EXPERIMENTAL SUBVERSIONS OF MODERNITY

1

Arthur Schopenhauer's great achievement was to find his way back to ancient truth through the modes and methods of modern philosophy. He was, in fact, the last of the great philosophers writing in the tradition of Platonism. Yet his role in this tradition is obscured by a consensus that situates him among the Post-Kantians. Schopenhauer himself encouraged this view by repeatedly stressing his indebtedness to Kant; also by insistently challenging the Kantian credentials of contemporary idealists, whom he regarded as utterly unfaithful to the great man's original insights. Today we think differently: we regard Hegel as Kant's major heir and Schopenhauer as just one of the many lesser lights of nineteenth century German idealism. As one among several Post-Kantians, Schopenhauer is inevitably overshadowed, particularly by Hegel and the tradition descending from him that influenced so profoundly the intellectual life of the twentieth century. This accounts for the near oblivion into which Schopenhauer's reputation has declined. If one proceeds from Kant directly to Hegel and his intellectual progeny, there is much to distract one from turning back to attend to Schopenhauer.

The few scholars who think and write about Schopenhauer often do so with Nietzsche in mind. They are really thinking and writing about Nietzsche, or preparing to write about Nietzsche, or publishing material gathered in the course of researching and writing about Nietzsche previously. We should not expect much of work produced in this manner; thus we shall not be disappointed. No significant biographical information has appeared since immediately following Schopenhauer's death. Regarding his philosophy, no one has surpassed Bryan Magee's twenty-five year old analysis. A few intrepid souls have made progress here and there by conducting scholarly researches into this or that nook of Schopenhauer's system, but they have made few substantive advances.

At the time of his death Schopenhauer was the most widely read philosopher in the West. He will never again receive his due unless we rethink his place in the history of philosophy.

The meaning and power of Schopenhauer's philosophy elude us because at the core of his system are two contrary and competing tendencies. The intellectual spirit of his guiding ideas descends from an era whose distance from the period of his philosophical activities is measured in millennia. Schopenhauer is an ancient and a modern simultaneously—or, to be precise, he is an ancient born into a world that taught him to think in a modern vocabulary. In order to appreciate fully Schopenhauer's fundamental insights, we shall have to regard his work as a continuation of ancient philosophy obscured by the fog of modernity. This is precisely the approach we adopt in this essay. But we also go further than this, for we aim at something more than a provocative analysis of Schopenhauer's system. Our goal is to recruit Schopenhauer into the ranks of premodern philosophers. Though he stands already with one foot on this side of the divide, we intend to bring him entirely into the premodern camp by replacing the modern elements of his system with an ontology derived from Platonism.

Two features of Schopenhauer's philosophy are responsible for its modern appearance: Kantian Transcendental Idealism and Enlightenment naturalism. According to Schopenhauer's version of Transcendental Idealism, the material world exists only as a representation in the mind of a knowing being; it is the phenomenological result of the way our perceptual and cognitive systems process the world as Will through the forms of space, time, and causality. This subjectivist account is incompatible with the Platonic understanding of the world as an objectively existent creature, manifestation, or emanation of a higher order of being. Transcendental Idealism is a particularly radical form of subjectivism, which is to say it is thoroughly *modern*. We must, therefore, eliminate or substantially revise this part of the system in order to classify the whole as genuinely *pre*modern.

Schopenhauer's naturalism operates on two levels: in his account of the empirical aspect of the world, it is manifest in his substitution of *brain* for Kant's *mind*. In his account of the world's transcendental character, it is manifest in his substitution of *Will* for a Platonic *Intellect* or *Soul*. This is not quite modern materialism, for according to Schopenhauer matter itself is phenomenal. Yet the system inclines toward materialism: since the empirical world as Schopenhauer conceives it is thoroughly material, if one rejects Transcendental Idealism, and thus also the transcendental aspect of the world—as we intend to do—only matter remains.

If Schopenhauer's Transcendental Idealism is a type of modern subjectivism and his naturalism is so close to modern materialism, what hope have we of casting his system in a premodern mold? We contend that these modern elements are merely *phenomenal* aspects of Schopenhauer's system, conditioned by the time and place of its production. The core of his system, its *noumenal* aspect, is the insight that ultimate reality is one, and that the objectification of this one is the material world around us. In short, Schopenhauer's system is a form of Platonism filtered through the distorting lenses of Kantian epistemology and Enlightenment naturalism. We intend to demonstrate this by stripping Schopenhauer's philosophy of its phenomenal modern elements while preserving its fundamental theses, which constitute the ancient noumena of his system. If we reject only the

Transcendental Idealism, however, the system will collapse into a modern materialism. If we reject only the naturalism, we shall be left with a thoroughly modern subjectivism. In neither case will we approach the premodern. We must, therefore, eliminate the subjectivism and the naturalism simultaneously. To accomplish this we shall have to ground the system on an objectivist metaphysics that derives the material world from an immaterial order.

Our Platonic reconstruction of Schopenhauer's philosophy will generate conclusions at odds with Schopenhauer's own, but the incompatibilities will surface only in reference to those parts of his system that are problematic as they are. This is not to say that the parts we intend to reject or revise are insignificant. They are not. Schopenhauer would no doubt complain that by altering them we disfigure his system beyond recognition. This may be, at least to the extent that one recognizes a thing by its appearance. But we are concerned less with appearance than with reality. We modify the appearance because the features that compose it are flawed, and by excising these blemishes we preserve the integrity of the thing itself. We put the knife to these parts of Schopenhauer's system also because they are modern. The imperfections at issue are the result of Schopenhauer's failure to be true to the ancient core of his thought, of his attempt to reach the ancient noumenon—ultimate reality is one—through modern phenomena—Transcendental Idealism and naturalism. By revising his system according to a Platonic ontology we shall be more faithful to Schopenhauer's fundamental insights than he was himself.

In general terms, and adopting a more or less standard account, we may summarize the ontology of Platonism as follows: Ultimate reality—metaphysical reality—consists of three fundamental substances, or hypostases: the *One*, the ultimate ground and source of all, is a simple and indivisible Unity prior to everything that is—prior in an ontological rather than a temporal sense (for the One is not subject to temporal predication; it is subject to no predication whatever); *Nous*, or *Intellect*, is the principle of being and essence, functionally equivalent to Plato's "realm" of the Forms; the *World Soul*, or simply *Soul*, is the principle of life that infuses and animates the universe; it is the progenitor of individual souls.

The One is beyond being, independent of the other two hypostases, Nous and Soul, which are ontologically dependent progressions or emanations of this unconditioned Source. Matter, and thus physical reality itself, is an emanation of Soul, or, to state the case more accurately, it is what results when the emanation deriving from Soul, and through Soul ultimately from the One, fades out. As such, matter borders on non-being. It *is* and *is not* simultaneously, which is to say it is less than fully real.

Each of the posterior hypostases emanates from and reverts to return to its prior, and each of these movements—emanation and return—is simultaneously a contemplative and a productive act. The One's self-contemplation gives rise to Nous. Nous, though the offspring of pure unity, is not itself a one; it is rather a one-and-many, a unity in and of plurality, a singular ontological principle of many Forms. The multiplicity within this singular hypostasis is a result of the inferiority that attends Nous' status as offspring—as posterior it is necessarily less perfect than its prior, the One; also of Intelligible Matter, which constitutes in Nous the possibility of plurality. As one, Nous has a unitary (mode of) knowledge of the One; as many, the content of its knowledge—the Forms—is multiple, even though the ground of this content—the One—is an indivisible unit.

The self-contemplation of Nous gives rise to the World Soul. The World Soul, as necessarily inferior to its progenitor, is not (as Nous is) a one-and-many, but rather a many-and-many, a multiplicity. One aspect of this multiplicity is the World Soul's multiple (mode of) knowledge, which results from the fact that each one of the many individual souls that are its offspring is a subject of its (i.e., the World Soul's) knowledge;[1] the other is the multiple content of this knowledge, namely the many individuals that are the objectifications of each one of Soul's many objects of knowledge—the universal Forms—the totality of these individuals comprising the experienced world of spatial, temporal, causally interconnected material particulars. In short, the World Soul's contemplation of Nous manifests as a multiplicity of souls contemplating the Forms, each Form appearing to each soul as a multiplicity of individuals. The result of all this activity is the material world familiar to us through sense-experience.

This précis of Platonic ontology supplies the terms we require to rethink Schopenhauer's system. For Schopenhauer's Transcendental Idealism, from which he derives the spatial, temporal, causally interconnected material world, we substitute the activity of individual souls, which, as subjects of the World Soul's contemplation of the Forms, know the material world of multiple particulars into existence. Our minds—and our perceptions of space, time, and causality—depend upon particular brains; here we agree with Schopenhauer. But as Platonists we must add that particular brains—and the spatial, temporal, and causal relations to which brains are necessarily posterior—depend upon souls, which as subjects of the World Soul's contemplation produce the material world and all the brains within it. In short, although minds depend upon brains, brains depend, through souls, upon Soul. Space, time, and causality are not *conditions* of Soul's—or of souls'—knowledge, as they are conditions of the brain's knowledge in the system as Schopenhauer presents it. They are rather

---

1. The idea is similar to Schopenhauer's thought, expressed in his essay "Transcendent Speculation on the Apparent Deliberateness in the Fate of the Individual," that the world is a dream of Will and that each individual is simultaneously a figure within this dream and a dreamer of the dream. The Will dreams *through* *us* as dreamers—we are the multiple subjects of the Will's one dream.

its *products*—constitutive features, not of Soul's cognitive apparatus, but of the world that Soul knows into being.

Individual souls are ontologically prior to brains, for brains are objects in the material world whose very existence is dependent upon and derived from the contemplative-productive activities of these souls. Thus, our Platonic revision of Schopenhauer's Transcendental Idealism necessarily undermines his empirical naturalism: there is more to reality than matter, and whatever reality there is in matter depends upon this more. Moreover, since the souls upon which nature depends are the offspring of the one World Soul, itself the offspring of Intellect, and ultimately of the self-reflective One, the revised system centers on that which resembles a conscious intellect more than a blindly impulsive Will. This undermines Schopenhauer's transcendental naturalism.[2]

Despite these apparently radical changes, our revision preserves what we have called the noumenal aspects of Schopenhauer's system. Replacing Transcendental Idealism with the productive activity of Soul preserves his idea that space, time, and causality are ontologically derivative, but in an objectivist rather than a subjectivist mode. The material world is objectively real (not just empirically real and transcendentally ideal, as Schopenhauer would have it), though it is less real than the three fundamental hypostases. And though we have eliminated Schopenhauer's naturalism, we have preserved his insight regarding the empirical world that the One is objectified in nature and is the inner essence and active "force" of all things, ourselves as well as planets, plants, and subatomic particles.

---

2. To be accurate, by eliminating Transcendental Idealism we undermine the distinction between the empirical and transcendental aspects of the world.

EXPERIMENTAL SUBVERSIONS OF MODERNITY

The features of Schopenhauer's system that we have identified as phenomenal generate tensions throughout the whole. We have just encountered one of these problem areas in passing, namely the apparent paradox of the material world's existence depending entirely upon the prior existence of a material brain. Schopenhauer attributed this "antinomy" to the identity of the empirical and transcendental aspects of the world, an identity that constitutes the metaphysical knot at the heart of reality. This did not satisfy Nietzsche, who, judging the antinomy a knot in Schopenhauer's system, ridiculed the philosopher's inability to see (or his refusal to admit) its fatal consequences. Fortunately, we need not adjudicate this dispute, for we avoid the problem altogether by abandoning Schopenhauer's Transcendental Idealism and naturalism.

For another example of this species of difficulty, consider Schopenhauer's account of the aesthetic experience, according to which an individual in the right circumstances may become a pure, will-less subject of knowledge in contemplation of a (Platonic) idea (i.e., a Form). In other words, aesthetic contemplation can liberate us from the constraints of Will so completely that we unite with Form in an act of pure intuitive knowledge. An attractive idea, no doubt. But is it consistent with the principles underlying Schopenhauer's system? We cannot help but wonder how one can become a will-less subject of knowledge if knowledge is wholly dependent upon the brain while the brain, regarded transcendentally, is an objectification of the universal Will, and, regarded empirically, is an organ exclusively in the service of a physical organism's will to live. If everything is Will through and through, there is no escaping either Will or willing.

Either Schopenhauer's description of aesthetic contemplation is merely an *as if* account, or something that we may legitimately call a (in fact *the*) subject of knowledge exists independently of any individual's brain, and thus independently of Will and willing. But Schopenhauer's ontology provides no place for a universal subject of knowledge: it cannot be Will; it is not one of the many particular brains, nor any part or subsection thereof; it is not a representation generated by our cognitive apparatus. It is none of these things; but according to Schopenhauer's ontology there is nothing else for it to be.

If Schopenhauer is right to say that the one eye looks out through us all, then his assertion that the thing-in-itself is Will must be incorrect. The subject of this one eye's vision must be a subject of knowledge, and so must be capable of knowing. It must, then, be in some sense intellectual, or essentially related to Intellect.

We can achieve the end that Schopenhauer's ontology denies him by grounding his aesthetics on an objectivist Platonic ontology. According to this revised account, one is already a pure subject of knowledge; one's task, as Plotinus repeatedly reminds us, is to identify with this part of one's being. Aesthetic contemplation can help one accomplish this. The contemplative sees through the particular to the Form, and in doing so identifies with his truer, higher self—his soul—which, as an intimate part or aspect of the World Soul, is continually engaged in contemplation of the Forms. During aesthetic contemplation the corporeality of things falls away, just as Schopenhauer claims, and there remains only pure subject of knowledge in communion with Form, a temporary unity that persists until one falls back into the material world. Thus, by employing a Platonic ontology we account for the aesthetic experience as Schopenhauer describes it without generating the inconsistencies that arise from the coupling of his description with his system as it stands.

Schopenhauer was proud of having derived from the conclusions of Kant's Transcendental Aesthetic the argument that since space and time are phenomenal, the conditions of plurality cannot affect the noumenon—the thing-in-itself—which must therefore be one. He was equally pleased that this insight coincides with the wisdom of the ancients, the Hindus in particular but the Platonists as well. What we find objectionable in Schopenhauer's philosophy is not the insight he shares with Hinduism and Platonism, but the assumptions he shares with Kant and his modern predecessors. These assumptions impede Schopenhauer's progress toward his ultimate goal; they generate too many inconsistencies. But our fundamental objection is not to the system's logical failings; we object more emphatically to its modernism.

Has our Platonic modification of Schopenhauer's system discarded elements that Schopenhauer considered indispensable components of the whole? It has; but we have eliminated these elements intentionally, for we deny that they are indispensable. If they are essential, they are essential only to the phenomenal aspects of the system. But the phenomena at issue (Transcendental Idealism and naturalism) depend upon the assumptions of modernity, which we reject. Our intention has merely been to suggest that the noumenal core of Schopenhauer's philosophy can survive this rejection.

2

Perhaps the only way we moderns can approach Platonism is as Pyrrhonists. We appreciate its beauty, its mysteries and astonishing depths. We admire it for the role it has played in history, intellectual as well as cultural history. Platonism inspires greatness; this much we acknowledge, if only grudgingly. Yet we cannot believe Platonism to be true. As children of modernity we believe nothing to be true; science perhaps, but even admitting this much we ascribe to science only a circumscribed and finite truth. Any system that aspires to attain and communicate grand metaphysical truths is to us incomprehensible, laughable, or dangerous. Platonism we usually classify as dangerous. As Nietzsche said, all great things wander the earth in monstrous form.

Still, there is something enticing about Platonism. Nietzsche, again, is witness to this. Platonism is a labyrinth that beckons one in, especially one fascinated by the dark promise of minotaurs to slay, or by the potential transformation resulting from the encounter, no matter who slays whom. We cannot hold ourselves aloof from Platonism; at a minimum, we are moved to account for the power it has exercised over so many formidable minds. To accomplish this we must at least be acquainted with the fundamentals of the system. Yet there are those among us for whom this minimal approach is insufficient. Such men are not satisfied by a merely external inspection; they believe that to observe from a distance an edifice as intricate as Platonism, to regard it as though through the eyes of a demolition engineer, is to fail to see the structure in its entirety, is to overlook the deep foundations, subtle interconnections, and the unfolding implications of the whole. These are the intellectual experimenters among us, men who believe that a thorough understanding requires identification.

Yet with genuine identification comes sympathy. To inhabit a *Weltanschauung* sincerely, to look out upon the world through the portals of its deepest assumptions, can be a profoundly transformative experience. This is especially true with a system possessing as many charms as Platonism, particularly when these charms are of the mellow as well as the terrifying varieties. Platonism is not just appealing; it is seductive. True, it is possible to inhabit the system without in the end and for good yielding to its charms. It is possible, but it is not easy. Platonism is more than just a beautiful fancy; it is a highly developed and sophisticated logos. As a system of beliefs, Platonism may very well be false. As a rational structure of conceptual nuance and logical rigor, it demands our respect, perhaps even our awe.

EXPERIMENTAL SUBVERSIONS OF MODERNITY

But there is more than the logos to recommend Platonism. We have denied that it is a beautiful fancy. Yet it *is* beautiful. If we modern skeptics and nihilists are unmoved by considerations of verisimilitude, then factors we may categorize under the heading of aesthetics must influence our judgment of its merits. Of any philosophy submitted for our consideration we must ask: does it manifest, communicate, or inspire beauty; does it move us to goodness or greatness; is it a deep well of insight and surprise or is it shallow and easily exhausted; in short, does it offer more profound challenges and more sublime rewards than its competitors? Measured according to these standards, Platonism has few rivals. The historical record is illuminated by an array of figures whose brilliance is the reflection of Platonism, from Plotinus to Schopenhauer. This is not to mention Plato himself, whom even Nietzsche, in one of his rare moments of honesty regarding the master, recognized as the most beautiful growth of antiquity.

Anyone drawn into the orbit of Platonism is vulnerable, whether his approach is motivated by a quest for sympathetic understanding, respect for the logos, or admiration of the beautiful. What from a distance seem to be groundless assumptions appear sound when considered up close and in context of the whole; objections previously persuasive ring hollow and strike one as irrelevant. Infused with the spirit of Platonism, one stands as if on a height, from which his previous perspective—his previous *life*—appears shallow, pallid, and dry.

Has such a man become a Platonist? Or is he rather entangled in what we might call Pyrrhonian Platonism, or Aesthetic Platonism—a Platonism poised over an abyss? But let us not follow Nietzsche down the alluring but impossible path of nihilistic affirmation. Those who attempt to dance over abysses inevitably fall to the bottom of their own dark wells. One may begin by regarding Platonism as an abyss, by leaping into the system motivated by a Nietzschean desire for intellectual exploration. But the man who does so will find that he does not fall, that he is supported, that beneath his feet there is no void, but rather solid and stable ground. And one day he will learn that his desire to plunge into murky abysses was naive and misguided to begin with—was, in brief, an expression of the decadence of modernity, for which the best remedy is the Platonism that now sustains him.

3

The Platonic philosopher seeks no longer to be a philosopher. He aspires to something beyond philosophy. In his case, however, *beyond* does not mean "after." That which comes *after* philosophy, after the life and death of philosophy, is decadence. Contemporary post-philosophical movements signify a world after philosophy in the direction of a descent. Positivism, Pragmatism, and Postmodernism follow philosophy, but not as its culmination or sublimation; they are products of the exhaustion of philosophical culture. The philosopher moves in a direction contrary to the trajectory travelled by the last men and misologists responsible for systems and anti-systems such as these. He pursues a goal that lies *prior* to philosophy along a path of *ascent*. Through purification he moves upward and backward: upward toward the One; backward toward a time—a time of mind, as it were—when there is no need to *seek* the One. Today our situation is such that we have need to find our way back to the One. Prior to and above philosophy is a place from which one need not go out in search of the One, for one is already (with) It.

4

It is no secret that Plato modeled his ideal polis, as outlined in the *Republic*, after what he knew of the Spartan constitution. The mystery is why he chose to do this. Plato's *Kallipolis* is oriented toward philosophy and the production of philosophers. The

Spartans were not philosophers. We do not ignore the fact that in the *Protagoras* Socrates attributes the Spartans' greatness to philosophical education (342A ff). We do not ignore the fact; but neither do we take it seriously, at least not according to its exoteric content. It is not that Socrates is lying; nor is he being ironical. He is being subtly devious.

In the *Protagoras* Socrates associates Spartan culture more closely with philosophy than with athleticism or militarism. He claims, moreover, that of all the Greek poleis, Sparta has the greatest concentration of sophists. It is odd, to say the least, for Socrates to identify philosophy and sophistry in this way; he is usually at pains to draw sharp distinctions between them. This is our first indication that he is being less than straightforward. Moreover, according to the implications of his own account, the Spartan intellect is neither philosophical nor sophistical. The Spartans, he says, are skilled in the formulation of concise and strikingly appropriate apothegms. He cites the maxims "Know thyself" and "Nothing in excess" as examples. But these laconic expressions do not amount to philosophy as Socrates elsewhere defines it, including in the *Protagoras* itself. They exhibit no dialectical precision or logical rigor. As for Sophistry: the Spartans' famous terseness, to which Socrates himself calls attention, reveals their distaste for the practice, which Socrates consistently associates with fatuous verbosity.

If the Spartans are neither philosophers nor sophists, what are they? Socrates provides a clue when he identifies the true source of their superiority as *wisdom* (σοφίαν, 342B6); also when he associates them with the Seven Sages (Σοφοί = *Wise* Men). We should not infer that Socrates believes Sparta to be a polis populated by wise men, for this is too bold a claim to make on behalf of so many individuals. Nevertheless, Socrates' remarks do imply that Spartan culture is founded upon wise principles and is, therefore, conducive to the development of wise men—indeed, Socrates

PURE: Modernity, Philosophy, and the One

includes the Spartan Chilôn in his list of the Seven. The Spartans, in short, are disciples of wisdom. They do not seek wisdom in the manner of a philosopher; they do not affect to possess wisdom in the manner of a sophist. They live wisely.

The Spartans occupy a cultural position prior to philosophy. They live in the light of wisdom, which must dim and blink out before philosophy can be seen, before philosophy can *be*. They have no need of philosophy because they possess a wisdom-tradition handed down from their ancestors, their sages, and their gods.

The philosopher inhabits a culture adrift from its tradition. He is a philo*sophos* rather than simply a *sophos* precisely because he must find his way back to forgotten wisdom.

The man unfortunate enough to have been born into a culture that has lost not only its wisdom, but also the memory of wisdom's previous existence, seeks nothing; or he seeks he knows not what. This is the source of sophistry and other forms of nihilism.

5

Nietzsche speculates that wisdom appears on earth as a raven drawn to the stench of cultural decadence. As always, he is *almost* right. The late-comer is *philosophy*; the carrion that attracts it is the rotting corpse of wisdom.

6

Philosophy is not a game; it is too serious to (de)merit this appellation. Yet there is something to the thought. We may say that the philosopher runs in circles if we are willing to add that wisdom is a sphere.

EXPERIMENTAL SUBVERSIONS OF MODERNITY

7

Manu, the first priest, sacrificed his twin brother Yemo, the first king. Having dismembered the corpse, he gathered up the pieces and from his late sibling's head created the sky; from his ear he made the four cardinal points; from his mind he made the moon, and from his eye the sun. This, according to the Proto-Indo-European myth of creation, is how the world began. This is the origin of the universe.

That sacrificer and sacrificed are siblings is significant; more significant still is the fact that they are twins. Twins exhibit a visible image of duality, but of a duality that is also a unity. Identical twins spring literally and directly from an underlying unity, a unity manifested in and through their duality so remarkably that the result can be unsettling. But even fraternal twins are suggestive of unity; indeed, the phenomenon strikes some minds as strange and portentous precisely because of the *simultaneity* of the dual births.

The symbolism of twins is naturally suited to the narrative representation of the dual activity of a single metaphysical principle. With this in mind, we can read the Proto-Indo-European creation story as encoding the belief that our cosmos arose from an original unity through a process of internal-division. The One became two and through this duality produced the many; or, to put it the other way around, material multiplicity sprang from the depths of metaphysical unity.

Manu, as the active agent of division, enacts the role of the One. The fact that he is a man symbolizes the One's intellectuality; that he is not just *a* man but *Man* symbolizes its *essential* intellectuality. The fact that Manu is a priest signifies the One's divinity; that he is the first and paradigmatic priest signifies the One's status as the All-divine. That this priest sacrifices a king represents the priority of metaphysical authority over temporal power.

In sum: at the heart of the Western world's foundational creation myth is the profoundly ancient belief that the source of physical reality is the metaphysical One, and that this One is a divine Intellect. In this we see the pre-Platonic life of Platonism.

8

The Platonic philosopher passes down a *way of life*; he transmits the inherited wisdom of ages. His ideas are not original. To him, originality is an objection.

9

Our Pragmatism: Older, truer.

PURIFICATION

1

Metaphysical truth is attained by and through logos—but logos is accessible only to the pure.

2

The church officials who refused to look through Galileo's telescope were guilty of willful ignorance. The phenomena he claimed to have discovered can only be experienced by way of this procedure. To reject his claims without employing the proper method is to violate all the canons of intelligent inquiry. Similarly, to dismiss metaphysical propositions before employing our only means of understanding and evaluating them is to be obstinately ignorant.

The greatest of the ancient and medieval metaphysicians taught that metaphysical knowledge is accessible only to those who practice purification (κάθαρσις, καθαρμός). Their conceptions of the process and the state of purification differ, but the variations are minimal. Most descend from Plato's *Phaedo* and emphasize the life of virtue. According to this tradition, the virtues are purifications; to acquire the virtues and to live virtuously are purificatory acts. The soul that has been purified through habituation to the intellectual and moral virtues is a soul prepared to receive metaphysical truth. There is no other way: if you want to see distant physical objects up close, you must employ a telescope. If you long to acquire metaphysical knowledge, your soul must be pure.

PURE: Modernity, Philosophy, and the One

The potential reward that awaits the purified soul—the intellectual insight and the existential state—is of the highest possible order, namely the realization of the human *telos*, which the Platonic tradition conceives as unification with the divine. Yet the sublimity of the goal is matched by the arduousness of its attainment. The acquisition and maintenance of the purificatory virtues require the consistent imposition of the strictest self-discipline over a period of years. The tug of the physical is immediate and powerful, impossible for many to resist. The rewards of submission to the body are paltry and base, but they are easy.

We moderns have been deprived of an education conceived on the Platonic model, an education designed to turn the soul away from its natural (in one sense of this word) obsession with the physical and toward the immaterial and metaphysical, the source and setting of all that is truly natural. We have lost contact with those ancient traditions that taught the purpose and reward of the life of purification. As a result of our ignorance we careen along the well-worn paths of empiricism and materialism, as physical objects travel along lines of least resistance.

No man will subject himself to the rigors of purification unless he understands something of the benefits of such a life. To understand this fully he must know what he is as (a) man (γνῶθι σαυτόν), which requires education in the deepest sense of the word. But this sort of education is already a form of purification. Genuine education and purification coincide, as education and virtue coincide. Only the pure soul is prepared for education; only the educated soul seeks purification. Is this a vicious circle? There is a circle here, to be sure; but it is an existential rather than a logical circle. We are describing a way of life, and the structure and course of a human life is not determined by the canons of logical necessity—which is not to deny that it is subject to other, perhaps deeper, sources of necessity.

PURIFICATION

In the *Phaedo*, Socrates insists that the man who adheres to the canons of what today we call empiricism and materialism, the man who determines truth according to the standard of the body, lives the worst possible life (83C–E). Presumably, Socrates—or Plato—arrived at this conclusion by observing the moral and intellectual lives of the materialists and empiricists he saw around him (also—and perhaps more importantly—from the tradition he inherited from the sages who preceded him). We can conclude the same for ourselves by observing the lives of our contemporaries. Modern modes of thought seem somehow to incline one toward vice, and thus toward a wretched existence.

But to condemn epistemological or ontological commitments based solely on the poverty of their existential consequences is to judge according to the standards of what Schopenhauer disparaged as "eudaimonism," by which he meant a doctrine that regards virtue merely as a means to an end. The end in this case is happiness, which is a worthy goal, especially happiness understood as eudaimonia. But eudaimonia is not our highest goal, nor should it supply our ultimate motivation. We should never diminish the virtues by assigning them the inferior status of means to some other end.

As Schopenhauer pointed out, of all the ancient traditions only Platonism transcended eudaimonism. The Platonic philosopher loves virtue because he loves the good; he loves the good because the good is divine. Eudaimonia as a life of virtue is a noble goal to which all humans should aspire. But the Platonist aspires to something more; he seeks a truth beyond the merely physical, a truth with which he can unite through contemplation. In short, he seeks to know the good and to be good because he aspires to participate in the divine. The real problem with reducing reality to the material and seeking truth exclusively through the body is metaphysical. The problem is the failure to Return, in a Platonic sense—to return, that is, to the One.

Purification facilitates this Return by liberating one from the reductive naturalism inherent in the modern worldview. Through purification one separates oneself from the body, which is to say one identifies oneself with the soul (and, through the soul, with Soul), directs one's attention toward and situates one's spiritual center in that part of one's being that transcends the body. Here is the source and residence of virtue. Here also is intellect. The act of separation—of *purification as separation*—is the practice of determining the true and the good by the standards of soul. The metaphysical, as Plato says, is not sensible; it is intelligible. Our body has no access to intelligible being. Only our soul has the potential to commune with the metaphysical, and we actualize this potential in no other way than through the practice of purification.

3

The ascendancy of modern science, of empiricism on one side and "the method" on the other, coincides with the rejection—or rather the neglect and forgetting—of purification as a prerequisite to knowledge. At the onset of modernity the search for knowledge was turned over to the senses and technique; the purificatory virtues dropped out. If only the physical is knowable, as long as the body is functioning properly one may ignore the soul. Even a criminal can operate a microscope.

4

If only the material realm exists, then properly functioning senses and "the method" are all we require to attain knowledge. If there is something more, something ontologically prior to the physical, then knowledge requires purification.

PURIFICATION

5

The idea of purification is ancient, even from the point of view of the ancients themselves. In its original form it served a variety of functions distinct from those that developed under the influence of Platonism. As originally conceived, purification was thought to cleanse one of the pollution (μίασμα) that attended certain acts: offenses against the gods, nearness to birth or death, engaging in certain types of sexual activity. Purificatory rites were also performed on regular occasions to ensure and preserve the sacredness of an event and the activities associated with it: before meetings of the assembly, for example, or prior to sacrifices and other ritual performances. Purification was practiced by physicians and seers as well, men whose intimacy with the divine enabled them to preserve or restore the health of individuals as well as entire cities. Purification as it concerns us here most likely descended from this last tradition, which included men—the Cretan Epimenides being perhaps the most famous—who combined the attributes of prophet, healer, mystic, and philosopher. Purificatory rites took various forms and were directed toward various ends, but they had in common the act of placing the human in a proper relation to the divine. This fundamental aim of purification was preserved for centuries, even when the practice was adapted to meet strictly philosophical ends.

Plato discusses purification at length in the *Phaedo*, yet nowhere in that work does he explicitly identify the goal of the process. There are a few indications, but the dialogue is ultimately concerned with other matters. Socrates discusses purification in the course of explaining and justifying his calmness in the face of death: he does not fear death, which is the soul's escape (ἀπαλλαγή) from the body, because the philosopher regularly undertakes his own version of this escape while living. In his pursuit of knowledge the philosopher directs his attention away from the many physical particulars in order to concentrate upon the metaphysical. The soul must be as independent of the body as possible in order to know true reality, the Forms, which are themselves independent of their corporeal instantiations. The philosopher attains independence through the soul's escape, which is simultaneously the act and the goal of purification. The purified philosopher, whose soul engages in its proper intellective activity independently of the body, approaches closer to true knowledge than those submerged in the whirl of the senses.

We know that the philosopher desires wisdom. The *Phaedo* teaches that one draws near to wisdom only through purification. Yet no one in the dialogue identifies wisdom *in this life* as the ultimate goal of purification. In fact, Socrates claims that we acquire pure knowledge only in Hades (66E–67B; 68A–B). Should we take him at his word? Is the aim of purification a state attainable only after death?

Early in the *Phaedo* Socrates expresses confidence that after death he will live among wise and good gods (63B–C), which expectation he re-characterizes as a confidence that after death he will acquire wisdom through pure knowledge of the Forms (66E–67C). Later, in the course of his second proof of the soul's postmortem existence, Socrates says that the soul that keeps itself apart from the body is akin to the pure and eternal realm, which it enters and "comes to be with always" (ἀεὶ μετ' ἐκείνου τε γίγνεται) so long as it keeps itself to itself (79C–D). After concluding his argument, he characterizes this state as being with the good and wise god in Hades (80D) and as passing one's time with the gods (81A). In a discourse immediately following this argument and just prior to his critique of empiricism, Socrates declares that those who have attained complete purity (παντελῶς καθαρῷ) through deliverance (λύσει) and purification (καθαρμῷ) will live among the gods after death (82B–D). Near the end of his remarks he once again modifies his account and redescribes the situation thus: through deliverance the soul will live

PURIFICATION

among, and acquire knowledge of, the divine, pure, and uniform (τοῦ θείου τε καὶ καθαροῦ καὶ μονοειδοῦς), which adjectives Socrates typically applies to the Forms (83A–E).

In each of these accounts Socrates employs the terms "god" and "true reality" interchangeably. This is his consistent practice: throughout the *Phaedo* he equates "to dwell with the gods" with "to dwell in the region of true reality." In the mythos near the end of the dialogue he maintains that the man who dies with a pure soul will in the afterlife live in a place befitting his soul's purity (108C), a region he associates with the True Earth, an earth that is pure and moving in purity (τὴν γῆν καθαρὰν ἐν καθαρῷ κεῖσθαι τῷ οὐρανῷ, 109B7–8). Dwelling thus apart from the body and in the purest realm of reality, the soul will have access to the wisdom that only the philosopher can attain, and only after death.

According to this reconstruction, Platonic purification is a sort of deliverance, a process of releasing the soul from the bonds of the body that has as its goal an association with and knowledge of true reality. Though one can approach this wisdom while alive, true and complete wisdom is reserved for the pure soul after death, which soul not only knows the Forms but in some manner dwells in and among them. Thus, when Socrates says that he hopes in the future to live among the gods, we should understand "gods" to mean "divinities," "divinities" to mean "Forms," and "Forms" to mean "true reality." But what exactly does it mean to say that the soul after death lives in true reality?

In the course of a long "digression" in the *Theaetetus* Socrates famously remarks that because evil characterizes this mortal realm we should escape as quickly as possible by becoming like god (ὁμοίωσις θεῷ, 176A–B). According to Socrates' account, one attains likeness to god by becoming just and pious with wisdom (δίκαιον καὶ ὅσιον μετὰ φρονήσεως, 176B1–2). He who has attained to likeness will after death enter the region pure of evils (ὁ τῶν κακῶν καθαρὸς τόπος, 177A5). Though the images differ from those in the *Phaedo*, the substance of the two accounts is similar. The resemblance is brought out even more when we note that Socrates' remarks in the *Theaetetus* appear in the course of his description of the philosopher as one who desires nothing so much as to attain reality (τοῦ ὄντος, 172D9) and who pursues the total nature of each of the wholes among real beings (πᾶσαν πάντῃ φύσιν...τῶν ὄντων ἑκάστου ὅλου, 173E6–174A1). This language, like the language in the *Phaedo*, implies an association, perhaps an *identity*, between divinity and true reality. To be with the gods, or to be like god, is to meet with, to dwell among, the Forms, the highest realities and the ultimate objects of knowledge.

Although the most famous passages concerning purification and assimilation to the divine occur in the *Phaedo* and the *Theaetetus*, these themes appear in other dialogues as well. In the *Phaedrus*, for example, during a speech that is itself an act of purification (ἐμοὶ...καθήρασθαι ἀνάγκη, 243A2–3), Socrates says that pure souls in the company of the gods enjoy a vision of reality as it is in itself, shining forth in pure light (ἐποπτεύοντες ἐν αὐγῇ καθαρᾷ, καθαροὶ ὄντες, 247B–250C). In the *Republic*, in which dialogue we learn that by associating with the divine the philosopher becomes as divine as is humanly possible (500C–D; see also 613A–B), those who have been educated properly are said to dwell in the pure (οἰκεῖν ἐν τῷ καθαρῷ, 520D8). Purification occurs even in a later and more prosaic work, the *Sophist*, in which dialectical refutation is described as the greatest and most effective of the purifications (τὸν ἔλεγχον λεκτέον ὡς ἄρα μεγίστη καὶ κυριωτάτη τῶν καθάρσεών ἐστι, 230D7–9). Purification thus described lacks the ecstatic, almost mystical quality of the *Phaedo*'s escape and deliverance from the body, but at bottom the two dialogues agree: purification purges the soul of false beliefs and thereby prepares it to receive the truth.

PURIFICATION

As suggestive as these accounts are, Plato never unambiguously characterizes the goal of purification as unification with the divine (as many later Platonists will do), much less as an act of unification available to the living. Yet this may have less to do with Plato's philosophical commitments than with the dramatic demands of the dialogues in which these topics appear. In the *Phaedo* the emphasis is on the afterlife, but this is conditioned by the dialogue's setting. The conversation takes place on the final day of Socrates' life; it is only natural that the philosopher's thoughts should turn toward death. Must we limit our reading to so narrow a context? May we not take the consequences of death as detailed in the dialogue as indicative of possibilities available to the living? We employ a similar interpretive strategy when we read Socrates' behavior in the face of his imminent execution as teaching the survivors how to bear themselves in life. The dialogue begins with the jailors delivering (λύουσιν, 59E6) Socrates' body from the bonds (τοῦ δεσμοῦ, 60C6) of the prison house shackles, which the attentive reader associates with the many later images of purification as affecting the soul's deliverance (λύσις) from the imprisoning bonds of the body (e.g., 67B–D, especially 67D1–2). This interplay between the imagery of escape through death and deliverance for the living is maintained throughout the dialogue. It appears also in the *Republic*, and in precisely those passages that address the soul's release from bonds *during this life* through education (515C4–5; 532B6). Though Plato's precise intentions must forever elude us, we cannot ignore the fact that his imagery, especially in light of the passages in the *Republic*, at least suggests that the soul's deliverance is available to the living through the appropriate philosophical practices.

Plato's philosophical descendents express themselves much more directly. This is particularly true of Plotinus, who unambiguously characterizes purification as a process leading to unification in this life, and who in doing so is confident that he is repeating what Plato had taught before him. In his most explicit account of the soul's encounter with the divine as the goal of purification, which he presents as an elaboration of Plato's ὁμοίωσις θεῷ, Plotinus plainly states that we desire not merely to be free of vice but to *be god* (θεὸν εἶναι, 1.2.6). This is accomplished, as is likeness to god in the *Theaetetus*, through a life of virtue. Here Plotinus elaborates upon Plato's account by identifying two categories of virtue, namely the civic virtues and the purificatory virtues. The former enable one to live a good life among one's fellow citizens; the latter lead one beyond mortal concerns to the realm of the divine—they prepare the soul for unification.

Plotinus returns repeatedly to this theme of unification, which is to be expected given his characterization of the first hypostasis as the One (τὸ ἕν). If the One is unity and nothing but unity, then to be like It one must become unity oneself; and to become actual unity rather than a mere image of unity one must unify with this One, for otherwise one would be oneself apart from the One, and thus at best a duality. According to Plotinus, then, Plato's likeness to god requires that one become god. But to become god is to become one with the One, to undergo unification. The prerequisite to unification is purification, for the One with which we aim to unify is the All-Pure (τὸ καθαρώτατον, 6.9.3). Only the pure can behold the pure, as like draws near to like.

Plotinus characterizes the act of unification in a number of ways. He writes, for example, of approaching the One; of having or becoming a vision of the One; of the divine appearing; of being taken up into the company of the gods—a multitude of images; yet, however varied, and regardless of the appearance of the words "god" or "gods," they are all variations on the theme of becoming one with the ultimate hypostasis that is beyond all gods, that is beyond Being itself. The *telos* of the philosophic life, which is the life of purification, is unification—τὸ ἑνωθῆναι. This is precisely how Porphyry described Plotinus'—and his own—

PURIFICATION

encounter with the divine. Four times during their acquaintance, Porphyry informs us, Plotinus unified with (ἑνωθῆναι) the ineffable and transcendent god.

Porphyry associates Plotinus' acts of unification with Plato's *Symposium* and *Republic*, which indicates his, and presumably his teacher's, belief that unification was precisely the goal toward which Plato's intellectual ascent through purification ineluctably leads. We have seen that Plato nowhere explicitly characterizes the process in this way. It may be that Plotinus modified Plato's account, at least as regards the possibility of unification during this life. Or, to repeat our earlier suggestion, perhaps Plato intended his descriptions of the life of the soul after death to serve as images of the rewards available to the man who while alive and dwelling upon the earth purifies his soul to such a degree that it moves somehow in an ontologically superior realm. Whatever we make of this problem, we may be sure that Plotinus would insist that his account was faithful to Plato's intent.

This conception of unification through purification, ultimately deriving from Plato, influenced the later pagan philosophical tradition as well as early Christian theology.[1] In the gospel attributed to Matthew, we read: "Blessed are the pure of heart, for they will see God" (5.8). Though there is no mention here of unification, the thought is nonetheless a succinct expression of one version of the nature and goal of purification. The emphasis on purity (οἱ καθαροί) recalls Plato; the vision of God (τὸν θεὸν

---

1. The medieval Islamic philosophers were influenced by this tradition as well, though with an admixture of Aristotle. Their understanding of Aristotle was itself shaped by Plotinus through the so-called *Theology of Aristotle*, which was actually a summation of the *Enneads*. Nevertheless, many of these thinkers were exercised by Aristotle's cramped account of the Active Intellect in Book 3 of *De Anima*, and it was with this Intellect, rather than with a Platonic One, that a thinker like Al-Fârâbi sought "conjunction" (*ittisâl*).

ὄψονται) looks forward to Plotinus. This is not to claim that the author of the gospel was a Platonist; his idea has roots in the Judaic tradition. Still, it is no easy task to disentangle the thought from the Platonic tradition, which by the first century AD had penetrated and influenced, either directly or indirectly, intellectual life all around the Mediterranean. Philo of Alexandria best represents the meeting point of Platonic philosophy and Jewish theology. For him, as for the author of the gospel, one approaches God along the path of virtue.

Plotinus' student Porphyry, whose use of the term τὸ ἑνωθῆναι we have mentioned, developed an elaborate account of the virtues' role in the process of unification (for which see his *Letter to Marcella* and *Launching Points to the Intelligibles*, §32). Iamblichus, Porphyry's student, applied the term henôsis (ἕνωσις) to his own version of unification. Iamblichus' practice of theurgy, a type of ritual magic intended to invoke the presence of divine beings, deviates from the purely meditative and contemplative practices Plotinus advocated. Nevertheless, his goal—to become one with the divine, hence *henôsis*—is clearly inspired by Plotinus' teachings regarding purification and its *telos*.

The Greek Orthodox tradition developed the idea of theôsis (θέωσις), the act of becoming divine, or at least of participating in the divine life and energies of God. Theôsis is a form of salvation, a process of actualizing one's full potential as a creature formed in the divine likeness. Accounts differ, as is inevitable in a tradition that covers such an expanse of time and space, yet there is a basic agreement that humans can, and in order to attain our true end *should*, aspire to a life of spiritual discipline and virtue—a life, that is, of purification—and thereby manifest the divine aspects of our nature. This is theôsis.

According to Catholic tradition, particularly as exemplified in the work of Thomas Aquinas, our true *telos* as human beings is the beatific vision, the direct vision of the essence of God. Aquinas agrees with Plato (or anyway with what Plato seems to say) that the vision is attainable only after death. The life of virtue prepares one for this vision, but even the most virtuous individual is incapable of beholding God during this life. As for the good of the still living human being, Aquinas agrees with Aristotle that we attain eudaimonia through contemplation of God. Still, embodied human contemplation is knowledge of the divine mediated through a finite intellect. After death we will encounter the divine essence as a disembodied immaterial soul beholding the immaterial source of all; we will—to employ Plotinus' formulation—gaze upon the divine as pure soul in communion with the All-Pure.

These Christian ideas eventually flowed back into their pagan sources through the efforts of Marsilio Ficino and his Platonic Academy in quattrocento Florence. Ficino's translations of Plato, Plotinus, and the Hermetic treatises—chimerical amalgams of Platonism, early Christian mysticism, and Egyptian magic, that everywhere call on man to realize and actualize his divinity—gave new life, if only for a short time, to the idea that man's *telos* is unification with the divine through purification. Although the onset of modernity ensured that this understanding of the human-divine relationship would never again receive the respect and acceptance accorded it in the ancient world, the tradition survives, most evidently in certain schools of Christian and Islamic mysticism.

Given the long history of the Platonic tradition and the breadth of its influence, we should not expect universal agreement regarding the details of purification and unification. Philosophers have struggled, with themselves and with one another, to arrive at precise formulations: does unification occur only after death or is it available to the living? Does unification mean likeness to god through a life of virtue, participation in the divine energies, or a merging of our soul with the divine essence? Must we actually *become* one with the divine or are we by nature already united with the source of our being and have only to realize and live in the awareness of this intimate bond? Such questions illuminate the layers of interpretative tensions and the substantive concerns that this tradition must continually address. But beneath the inevitable differences and disagreements there is a consensus, maintained for more than two thousand years, that the human being is in some way bound up with the divine source of all being, that his fullest life consists in contemplating and actively participating in the outpouring energy of this divinity, and that this life can be achieved only through the disciplined practice of purification.

6

The several modes of purification:

Physical purification: On the hierarchy of being and value soul stands higher than body. Physical purification is a procedure whereby an untrained, undisciplined, uneducated body is made to submit as a slave to the soul as master. But this is only the initial stage of the process: ultimately, the body should learn to act as a disciple of the soul as teacher. When this state is achieved, body and soul work in harmony to the benefit of each.

Physical purification acts on the body, but not for the sake of the body alone. The primary goal is not physical fitness. As in all forms of purification, the object of the process is the health of the soul. We must purify the body because its condition affects the soul, at least to the extent that an unhealthy body responds sluggishly or defiantly to the soul's direction. By consistently subjecting the body to the discipline applied by the soul, we reinforce in ourselves a vigilant awareness of their relative merit and worth (which is itself a reminder of their rank on the ontological hierarchy). We also habituate the body to its subordinate position and

PURIFICATION

thereby eliminate, or at least diminish, its inherent tendency to disturb or rebel against its superior.

Seen from the outside, physical purification resembles the sort of physical exercise with which we are all familiar. One runs, trains, eats well, drinks alcohol in moderation or not at all. In short, one consistently strives to maintain the body in peak physical condition. This qualifies as purification if one trains not for combat, for a marathon, or for any other competition of physical strength and endurance, but rather for the sake of the discipline to which the body becomes accustomed through this training; also if one instills this discipline for the still higher goal of producing a body that acts effortlessly as an emissary of the soul, a body conditioned to carry out the souls' decrees without irresolution or error. Such a body is in "peak physical condition." The body trained simply for itself, the body conditioned exclusively to run at high speeds or to lift heavy objects, may very well be unhealthy according to this standard. Our aim in training the body should be the production of a physical state conducive to the smooth functioning of the soul. The body's ability to perform physical feats is of secondary or tertiary importance. Moderation is knowing when to stop as well as when to begin.

Physical purification correctly administered produces a body that neither rebels against the soul's authority nor impedes the implementation of its intentions. It liberates the soul to perform its own proper functions without the nuisance of bodily interference. In this way the soul benefits itself by improving the body. But physical purification is productive of more than an environment favorable to the soul's unhindered exercise of its powers. By imposing discipline on the body the soul disciplines itself. It habituates itself to the virtues of consistency, perseverance, and courage. An untrained body is a restive beast, always straining against authority. It is lazy, graceless, and weak; the exertions of strenuous effort do not please it. It wants to rest and relax; it always wants to relax.

Here is the soul's great challenge, for it must learn to be hard. It must refuse to yield to the body's inevitable complaints and lamentations; it must develop an unwavering resolve based upon a confidence in its natural authority.

We all struggle against the contumacy of the body. Our body under stress, whether suffering from exhaustion or merely from boredom, is inclined to plead for a respite. Runners in particular are familiar with the internal voice urging them to rest, even when they have the stamina to continue. This voice indicates that physical fitness is as much a test of soul as of body. When the body begins to relax—and one may even feel it actually in the act of coming to a stop—the soul must drive it forward. But to do so the soul must rouse itself, for the soul too can grow weary. The body can do nothing without the soul's consent; it can rest only if the soul allows it to share in its own rest. Lethargy is a vice of the soul. The soul, as the seat of authority, must condition itself to exercise the power inherent in its station.

The soul that has disciplined itself in this way exhibits a virtue similar to courage as defined in Book 4 of the *Republic*. This variety of courage is the soul's preservation of the decrees of reason in the face of temptation or fear. Temptation and fear spring from bodily desires and anxieties. Once the soul has determined the appropriate course of action, it must steel itself against irrational bodily appeals. The body can be persuasive; it can be seductive. In the right circumstances, it can dominate a weak soul. The soul by nature is more authoritative than the body, but it is not always more powerful. It must grow strong, stronger than the body, which it accomplishes by consistently exercising its authority. As we have said, the body cannot disobey the soul without the soul's consent. By habituating itself to withhold this consent the soul conjoins power to its authority. Thus empowered, it trains the body more effectively, eventually producing a body no longer inclined to disobey.

PURIFICATION

The soul and the body act mutually upon one another, for better or for worse. The body degenerates under the regime of a vicious soul; a degenerate body impedes the soul's activities; a soul constrained in this manner declines even further from its proper virtues and eventually becomes impotent to check the decadent impulses of a disobedient body. Thus do the body and soul drag one another down. On the other hand, a virtuous soul trains the body well; a well-trained body is obedient to the soul's commands; a soul untroubled by bodily recalcitrance has greater liberty to deepen its commitment to virtue, which enhances its ability to train the body. In this way body and soul improve exponentially.

Physical well-being, health, and strength benefit the body, in itself and in its relation to the soul; they also benefit the soul, in itself and in its relation to the body. This is as true of the process of becoming fit as of the state of being fit. Knowing this, the philosopher regards physical fitness as a form of spiritual purification, and he exercises in order to produce—to paraphrase Porphyry—a pure body in the service of a pure soul.

Schopenhauer says that a man attains intellectual maturity at forty. Plato's assessment is similar, though less specific. In Book 7 of the *Republic* he assigns the duty of philosophical rule to men and women over the age of thirty-five and reserves the highest levels of philosophical education to individuals over fifty—men and women, it is worth noting here, who have exhibited physical as well as intellectual virtue. Plato's ancestor Solon, the great sixth-century poet and legislator, one of the Seven Sages, maintained that between the ages of forty-two and fifty-six a man's intellect is at its zenith. He, too, understood the relevance of physical conditioning: he lamented that although the mind remains sharp even into the seventh decade, the body's inevitable decline hinders its full expression.

Physical purification is a prophylactic against the threat of an aging body's precipitous decline. It is indispensable in the early years as well, for it prepares the body for the era of the intellect's maturity. The body is a vehicle for the expression of intellect; we must train it to be worthy of the intellect at its best. Wisdom may come with age; but it will not come to, or anyway it cannot be expressed in its fullness by, a physiologically degenerate man.

Ethical purification: The eye, to see, must be adapted to the object of its vision. So, too, with soul: only the good may know the Good; only the pure may know the All-Pure. Ethical purification is the process through which we become virtuous, for the sake of virtue itself, but also, and ultimately, for the sake of our ascent to the divine. We seek metaphysical insight, knowledge of Truth, unification with the One. This is a daunting goal; perhaps we are presumptuous to aim so high. Nevertheless, we are moved to make the attempt. We have been told, after all, that this is the *telos* toward which our human nature inclines. Therefore, it is not impossible. Yet it is not easy, this we have also been told. If, then, we would undertake the journey sincerely, we must follow the road tradition has laid down for us. The road is under our feet, and its paving stones are inscribed with instructions on how to proceed. We must walk, they say, with virtue.

Contemporary society impedes the practice of virtue and promotes vice. It works at this business so assiduously that one may be forgiven for suspecting the presence of a conspiracy dedicated to preventing us from actualizing our *telos*. Yet the members of such a cabal would have to know of this *telos*, its meaning and its function in relation to human nature. It is hard to believe that modern men in significant numbers are aware of these old truths; harder still to believe that a sufficient number of those who know would prefer to dissipate their energies obstructing others from reaching this goal than to work to attain it themselves. There *may be* a conspiracy; but if there is, it is a conspiracy of the ignorant.

PURIFICATION

There are powerful forces contriving to encourage vice in our society, but they have no more conscious intention than the selfish accumulation of material wealth and power.

However ignorant the merchants of vice may be, we require discipline to resist their influence, the discipline of active and alert observation. Note the many avenues from which the seductions to vice approach. At the root of vice are unnecessary desires, which Plato defined as desires we can eliminate with discipline and concentrated effort and which, moreover, do us no good and may even harm us. The young are most susceptible to the influence of these desires, and thus most vulnerable to their manipulation. This explains our culture's relentless deification of the young. Those who promote vice through the mechanisms of culture appeal to the vanity of the young in order to seduce them; they seduce them in order to molest them. The survival of these purveyors of vice depends upon the presence of a populace willing to provide them the sustenance that fuels their decadence. Therefore, they devise techniques to create individuals who identify so thoroughly with the circumambient culture that in supporting it they imagine they are supporting themselves. The young are the easiest prey.

If modern culture, or rather the individuals who live off its spoils, depend upon the vulnerable young, it is in their interest that the youth population be as large as possible. There is a limit to the natural production of children, determined by population numbers and the resources available to sustain new generations. Yet this limitation can be overcome by inducing those who are not by age actual members of the youth contingent to feel, think, and act as if they are. The relevant factor is not biological age, but unconstrained unnecessary desires. The more individuals the culture-industry can persuade to retain their adolescent attitudes and behaviors into biological maturity, the broader the market for the products of popular culture. This is another reason for our deification of youth. We are taught to regard the young as divine so that we will cling to our youth forever. Unfortunately, in this context "to cling to our youth" means "to still be vulnerable to the manipulation of our unnecessary desires."

To attain virtue, and through this simultaneously to attain the divine, we must decline to participate in the modern promotion of vice through the meretricious allurements of youth culture. We must situate ourselves in an oppositional relation to this culture. This is not to say that we should insistently regard our surroundings through the bars of this opposition. Opposition, too, can be a prison. We must not attend too closely to the baser elements of this world, to the fetters that bind us whether we are caught in them or free but obsessing about them. We require vigilance and prudence. Vigilance, to recognize the myriad schemes developed over generations to ensnare us; prudence, to identify the appropriate means of evasion or escape. Yet we must acquire these virtues properly and thoroughly, which is to say that we must attain a state in which we are vigilant and prudent without the need of constant attention. Having attained such a state, we may turn our minds toward more serious matters. We may turn toward our souls, and through them to Soul, and through this, of course, to the divine.

Uneducated desires focus almost exclusively on bodily pleasure. Bodily pleasure is produced by material means. Therefore, the more we chase after pleasure, the more firmly we bind ourselves to the material order. We attend to the corporeal to the exclusion of everything else. In time, we cannot believe in anything else. The body is all we see; the body is all we know. For us, the body is all there is and all there can be. What has become of the divine? Either the divine does not exist, or we ourselves—we ourselves in our glorious corporeality—are divine, which is just another and cruder form of atheism.

PURIFICATION

Virtue is the antidote to this condition. This conception of virtue informs ethical reflection within the Platonic tradition. It motivates, for instance, Plotinus' words at the end of his famous treatise on Beauty: To attain the Beautiful, which is also the Good—which is, in fact, the divine—we must look to the beauty and goodness inside ourselves. If we are neither beautiful nor good, we must make ourselves so, as a sculptor beautifies a statue. We must remove (ἀφαίρε) the superfluous (i.e., unnecessary desires) and purify (καθαίρων) that which is darkened (i.e., the soul lost in a fog of materiality) until a godlike splendor of virtue shines forth from within. Vice obscures our intimacy with the divine; it blinds us to our true nature, to the Truth in which we participate by nature. Virtue illuminates the darkness that we may see the Source of all illumination. Having become pure, we are prepared for the vision of this Source. We behold the divine by becoming godlike ourselves.

The idea that virtue is a prerequisite to the vision or knowledge of god is common to Platonists of all times and places; it amounts to saying that the virtues are themselves purifications. Plato says precisely this in the *Phaedo* (69C1–3), and Plotinus expands on the point in his treatise on the virtues (1.2). The virtues make one like god; we are familiar with this thought from Plato's *Theaetetus* (176A–B). But how, exactly, does virtue accomplish this? The divine is not virtuous: virtue is a state of the soul, but the divine has no states. The divine is the unchanging source and archetype of virtue, which is to say it is related to virtue in a manner unavailable to humans. This is true; nevertheless, we may liken ourselves to the divine according to the mode appropriate to human nature.

The soul is removed from its own proper act to the degree that it identifies with the body and its desires. The soul thus affected is vicious (κακή, 1.2.3), which is to say it is not itself; it has entered into an alien condition. The virtues liberate the soul from the corporeal realm, returning it to its natural state. *Return* is the appropriate word, for every embodied soul has fallen into impurity. Indeed, the soul's embodiment is the expression of this impurity. The virtues raise the soul up from its fallen condition by orienting it toward the divine, which is always present but often obscured by the pressures and exigencies of the body.

Ethical purification disciplines the body. Yet it does not mindlessly oppose the body. The virtuous man gives the body its due. The problem is that the body often demands *more* than its due. On these occasions the virtuous man does indeed oppose the body's unnecessary desires. But to oppose the body's irrational impulses is not to oppose the body itself. To the contrary, it is to cooperate with the body in the attainment of its best possible condition.

Ethical purification, like physical purification, operates on the body indirectly through its influence on the soul. Virtue is a condition of the soul, and to practice the virtues—even to attempt to practice them—is to train the soul by directing it toward its best possible state. Consider a Platonic understanding of the canonical virtues: wisdom, justice, temperance, and courage. Wisdom is the knowledge of what is good for the whole individual: body, soul, and each of their parts and aspects; justice consists in each part of the soul—reason, passion (or "spiritedness," θυμός), and the appetites—standing in a proper relation to the others; temperance is the harmonious maintenance of this order; courage is the soul's abiding by the dictates of reason, even in the face of temptation or fear.

We concentrate on soul because on the hierarchy of being and value soul is superior to body. The man possessed of the virtues in the genuinely Platonic manner orders his life accordingly. He rises above the narrow concern for corporeal well-being. He is in pursuit of metaphysical knowledge—he is in pursuit, ultimately, of unification with the divine. Though he seeks eudaimonia, he seeks something else besides. Though he knows that some pleasures are good, he has learned to enjoy the pleasures that attend good acts rather than to judge acts good according to the pleasures they produce.

The pure are motivated by something more than excellence or pleasure. The pure are virtuous because virtue is good and the good is divine—and the divine, in the end, is our one true goal.

Intellectual purification: Modernity existed even among the ancients. Plato was aware of the phenomenon and warned against it. He called it the greatest and most extreme form of evil. It is no coincidence that his one sustained critique of the intellectual assumptions of modernity and his most explicit account of purification appear in the same dialogue, the *Phaedo*. Purification is the cure for the disorder we call modernity.

The *Phaedo*, which on the surface concerns the immortality of the soul, is at its core a portrait of the premodern mindset. Socrates himself notes that his arguments for immortality are incomplete and dubious, at least as he has presented them (84C; 107B). The arguments are not his main concern; they are not Plato's main concern. Plato may very well have believed the soul to be immortal, and he may have thought that he could prove it. Yet he does not present his proofs in the *Phaedo*, at least not in the fullness of their development. He proceeds rather by implication and intimation. He provides the beginnings of arguments, preliminary proofs; he examines a few of the concepts that an exhaustive account of the human soul must include. But more than this, he illustrates a way of being—a way of thinking and a way of living—that is receptive to a logos that admits of an immortal human soul. The message of the dialogue is not, "since x is the case and y is the case, the soul is immortal;" but rather, "*this* is the look and feel of a world in which immortal souls have their place, and *this* is the mind of a man who inhabits such a world."

Plato sets the scene with references to divinity, purity, and deliverance from the body. We learn early in the dialogue that Socrates avoided execution for some time after his conviction because the Athenians were committed to maintaining a state of purity during the period of their annual embassy to Delos, birthplace of Apollo. When Socrates' friends arrive at his cell on the morning of the day of his death, the jailors are delivering the philosopher from his bonds (λύουσι, 59E6; λελυμένον, 60A1). Deliverance (λύσις) is associated with purification throughout the work, as philosophy is associated with death. From the beginning we see Socrates being delivered in preparation for his death. His body is delivered from the bonds of the prison house as his soul will be delivered from the prison house of his body. While awaiting his death, he discusses the life of purification that is prerequisite to philosophical deliverance. Socrates' examination of this life is just one of the many ways that he lives it.

According to Socrates' account, the philosopher strives to deliver himself from the body to facilitate both the practice of virtue and the search for knowledge, for neither virtue nor knowledge is properly related to the physical. Deliverance in this context is the act of freeing oneself from the tyranny of bodily desires, pleasures, and pains. It involves relocating one's spiritual center of gravity from the abdomen or groin to the head. One achieves deliverance through the practice of purification (καθαρεύωμεν, 67A5; κάθαρσις, 67C5), which in and of itself is the act of turning away from the body toward the soul. Purification—deliverance through purification—is a form of preparation (παρασκευάσηται, 65E3; παρεσκευάσθαι...κεκαθαρμένην, 67C2-3): by delivering the soul from the bonds of the body (ἐκλυομένην... δεσμῶν ἐκ τοῦ σώματος, 67D1-2) purification prepares the soul to receive that which is pure. Knowledge and virtue are pure. They are, in fact, purifications themselves (κάθαρσίς... καθαρμός, 69C1–3). But more pure still is true reality, the intelligible cosmos, which near the end of his discourse Socrates associates with the Earth in its ontological fullness. To reside here and to commune with the divine is the natural end, the *telos*, of human existence. The practice of philosophy as purification makes this possible. It delivers one from the constricting bonds of the physical Earth into the pure ether of the True Earth.

Philosophy = purification = deliverance (82D5–6). One implication of this equation is that philosophy is necessarily opposed to the reductivist naturalism inherent in modernity. At a minimum, it is suspicious of the modern inclination toward empiricism and materialism. But Plato advocates something more than mere suspicion. That his critique is more radical than this becomes evident in Socrates' account of the intellectual-existential attitude that he characterizes as "the greatest and most extreme of all evils" (πάντων μέγιστόν τε κακῶν καὶ ἔσχατόν, 83C2–3). The phenomenon to which he refers is the philosophical (rather, the *anti*-philosophical) position that we have identified as modernity.

Socrates had commented on the strange powers of pleasure and pain after the jailors released him from his bonds (60B–C). Reflecting now on the release achieved through philosophy—i.e., deliverance—he returns to the subject. The body, he observes, is so affected by pleasures and pains that men tend to believe that whatever induces these sensations is most real and most true (ἐναργέστατόν…ἀληθέστατον, 83C7). Our experiences of pleasure and pain can be powerful indeed; the sensations reverberate throughout our bodies, penetrating at times to what at least appear to be the very depths of our being. Bodily experiences this profound, Socrates suggests, can exercise an influence even upon one's soul. They can, as it were, bind soul and body together. In other words, bodily sensations can disorient the soul to such an extent that it adopts for itself the body's modes of evaluation. In the extreme case, it may even come to believe that truth is whatever the body says that it is. This is an intellectual disorder. The condition, as harmful as it is in itself, typically develops into an

PURE: Modernity, Philosophy, and the One

existential disorder equally injurious, a condition under the influence of which the soul shares contentedly in the body's preferred mode of living. This is a reversal of the natural hierarchy, according to which the body should yield to the authority of soul. This disordered state, ultimately caused by the body and its desires, is impurity.

The soul whose intellect and affect are impure cannot grasp that which is divine and pure (τοῦ θείου...καθαροῦ, 83E2) in itself, neither in this life nor in the afterlife, for the impure may not attain to the pure (67B2). But this is to say that the impure soul is incapable of achieving its highest goal. Worse, it is unable even to recognize the existence of this goal. It is precisely this condition, this abysm of intellectual and existential degeneration, that Socrates pronounces a great evil.

Notice that, according to Socrates' account, the soul is rendered impure by intellectual commitments familiar to us under the names *empiricism* and *materialism*. Pleasures and pains are sensible phenomena. He who takes bodily sensations to be the arbiters of truth is an empiricist. He who confines his ontology to that which is accessible only to the senses is a materialist. But empiricism and materialism are two of the defining features of modernity. The message of the *Phaedo*, then, is that modernity is pernicious. More, it is the worst possible state into which a man can descend. It distorts his intellect and impoverishes his life. Imprisoned in the bonds of physicality, the man committed to the assumptions of modernity is closed off from the metaphysical, which is the home of all that is true, good, and beautiful.

As if this were not reason enough to be wary of modernity, Plato expands his critique by associating the modern worldview with a phenomenon he identifies as misology, i.e., the hatred or mistrust of logos, which we may translate here as rational argumentation. Immediately following the critique of modernity, two of Socrates'

PURIFICATION

interlocutors raise objections to his proofs of the soul's immortality. Their arguments appear so cogent that some of those present begin to doubt Socrates' arguments, by which they had previously been persuaded. The uncertainty throws them into despair. Socrates of course intends to rebut the objections, but before doing so he addresses a vital preliminary matter: he warns his interlocutors against misology. Misology, he explains, is a condition that afflicts those who lack expertise in logos. These neophytes are vulnerable to the sort of rhetorical manipulation that persuades them to trust an argument at one moment and to doubt it the next. Repeated experiences of this kind can shatter one's confidence in reason altogether. One comes to believe that there is nothing either sound (literally, healthy: ὑγιὲς, 90C3) or certain in logos, but that all matters are subject to fluctuations of opinion and judgment. This attitude, which we recognize as a symptom of relativism or nihilism, is destructive of intellect. The misologist, presented with a sound argument, cannot recognize its conclusion as true. He mistrusts all arguments because he has decided that they are by nature unsound. His is a rash judgment, for he has ignored the possibility that he himself is unsound (unhealthy). This is a perilous mistake, for it prevents one from acquiring knowledge of anything other than bare physical reality.

The metaphysical is intelligible, not sensible. It cannot be grasped by the body, which reaches out to reality through the senses alone. Metaphysical knowledge is attainable only by and through logos. He who distrusts or dismisses logos admits of no mode of cognition higher than that generated by the deliverances of his senses. Such a man can learn nothing of a reality superior to the physical. But this is to say that the misologist is an empiricist.

The empiricist tends to measure the real according to the standards of the knowable. If it cannot be known, it is not real. The inference is fallacious, but it is common. Because our senses inform us of nothing other than material reality, the misologist-empiricist is likely to constrict the field of what he judges to be real and admit only the corporeal into the category of being. In short, the misologist is likely to be a materialist as well as an empiricist.

If these are the inevitable results of misology, then the misologist turns out to be the very man whose commitment to empiricism and materialism Socrates previously denounced. This explains why he remarks that there is no greater evil one can suffer than misology (οὐκ ἔστιν...μεῖζον...κακὸν, 89D2–3). Has he not already identified the greatest of evils, namely the empiricist-materialist perspective? Indeed, he has (83C2–3). The repetition is deliberate. Plato intends for his reader to identify these three phenomena. Misology, empiricism, and materialism are one. They are united under the banner of modernity, which banner signifies a regime of unparalleled evil. The lesson of Socrates' remarks is that a man can suffer no worse fate than to have his soul warped by the unsound doctrines characteristic of the modern worldview.

Against the threat of this disorder, Socrates advises caution. Rather than doubt the power of logos, the responsible thinker will ensure that he himself is healthy (ὑγιῶς ἔχειν, 90E3). He will strive to prepare his soul to receive the truth if he encounters it, for it is a great misfortune to be deprived of knowledge and the truth about reality. Worse still to deprive oneself by failing to diagnose and heal one's unhealthy soul (90D). "Healthy" in this context is another word for *pure*. The healthy soul, the soul receptive to knowledge and truth, the soul capable of attaining its highest goal and final end, its *telos*, is the soul that has been disciplined by purification.

At the center of the *Phaedo* beats an anti-modern, or rather a *pre*modern heart, whose rhythm radiates the following lesson: to attain metaphysical truth one must resist the intellectual assumptions of modernity (i.e., empiricism, materialism, and misology); to resist modernity one's soul must be healthy; a healthy soul is a pure soul; purity results from purification, which is the practice of philosophy as a disciplined way of life that everywhere yields to the authority of the natural hierarchy of being and value.

These reflections suggest, at the very least, that we should undertake the experiment of subjecting our modern intellectual assumptions to serious and sustained examination. They suggest, moreover, the complimentary act of conducting this examination by abandoning empiricism and materialism in favor of a premodern perspective. But is this possible? Can we moderns actually escape the intellectual paradigm in which we have been reared and educated? Perhaps it is impossible to escape completely; it is difficult to say. We will never know unless we make the attempt. Besides, escape—deliverance—is what we are after. We must, therefore, at least commit to the experiment.

Perhaps the best way to begin is simply to alter our manner of speaking. Whenever we converse or debate, with ourselves as well as with others, we should draw upon the conceptual and logical apparatus of a premodern worldview. We should, for example, speak from the perspective of Platonism. We have read the best of the Platonists; we are familiar with their central concepts and standard lines of argumentation. Let us imitate them. At first, imitation is all we will be able to manage. With time, however, their way of thinking will become our own, or anyway more and more like our own. Gradually, we will inhabit their worldview with some degree of intimacy. We will habituate ourselves to reason according to new standards, or rather according to ancient standards, standards that Plato might have included under the heading ὁ παλαιὸς λόγος, perhaps even ὁ θεῖος λόγος.

This very experiment is a mode of intellectual purification. It is one of the very few means we moderns have of purging ourselves of the intellectual presuppositions we have inherited from the past five hundred years of philosophical history. Yet we must be careful not to take our experiment in intellectual purification to such an extreme that we *beg the question* in favor of metaphysics. Intellectual purification involves correct belief, to be sure. But we must not simply advocate the groundless substitution of a premodern metaphysical perspective for the assumptions of modernity. This would parallel the fallacy that many ancient Platonists attributed to some of the early Christian intellectuals who attempted to incorporate purification into their theology. It is not necessarily question-begging to assert that knowledge of the divine requires an anterior belief. It depends upon one's understanding of belief. Plotinus and his students found a place for belief (*pistis*) in their system. But *pistis* in this tradition (which differs somewhat from *pistis* in the *Republic*) is a cognitive state attendant upon demonstration; it is not a groundless belief deriving from authority, hope, or desire. Groundless belief is precisely what the Platonists objected to in the theology of the early Christians, who commended to their coreligionists a *pistis* unmotivated by rational considerations, or at least unsupported by rational demonstration. This is *pistis* as faith. To seek knowledge of y by accepting x on faith, when x is so bound up with y as to be equally uncertain, is at best a problematic procedure; at worst it is an outrageous fallacy. Platonic philosophy differs from some manifestations of early Christian theology by conceiving of and employing *pistis* in a manner that avoids this fallacy.

The Platonists were subtle dialecticians, following the example of Plato himself, who never simply begs the question in favor of his own metaphysical system. In the *Phaedo*, for example, Plato advocates a philosophy of purification by exposing our inclination to beg the question in favor of the rival position. In this way he encourages us to evaluate our options without bias. The evaluation can remind us that the modern paradigm has no legitimate claim to an anterior status as the default position, the evidently superior philosophy in the face of which all competitors must assume the burden of proof. To realize this is itself a form of deliverance. It liberates one to regard Platonism as a living alternative. This is the beginning of purification.

Spiritual purification: Whether or not the ancient Greek philosophers practiced or taught meditation techniques is a matter of controversy. Most scholars deny it. Yet the ancient texts contain passages suggestive of related spiritual exercises. The accounts of Socrates' tendency to lose himself in thought and stand rooted to the spot for minutes or hours on end are evidently based upon the philosopher's actual practice of a type of silent stillness that was striking to those who observed it (*Symposium*, 174D; 220C–D). When Plato relates the ecstasy of rising in thought to a vision of ultimate reality, we seem to be reading the words of a man acquainted with experiences somehow greater than the modest enjoyment of philosophical conversation and dialectical disputation. Plato regularly employs visual imagery to portray encounters with truth, and his accounts are so vivid that we wonder whether he experienced such visions himself. The Greek word for contemplation, *theôria*, literally means a seeing, a beholding. Consider the sight beheld by the man possessed by the mad love of beauty in the *Phaedrus* (249D–250C), by the man who mounts the ladder of love in the *Symposium* (209E–212B), or by the man who ascends from the cave in the *Republic* (514A–517C): are we dealing here with highly wrought metaphors for knowledge acquired through the normal modes of experience or education, or are these images faithful depictions of the inner life of contemplation practiced according to the Socratic model of silent stillness? It may be that the word "meditation" is inapposite in this context, that we would do best to retain the Greeks' own terminology and speak instead of "contemplation." But it would be equally misleading to interpret this word according to the standards of modernity. We cannot believe that by "contemplation" Plato meant merely "the act of continuous and concentrated thinking; study," or some equally mundane practice. The dialogues are replete with references to initiation rites and mystery religions, prophecies received through dreams and oracles, divine inspiration, bacchic frenzies, descents and ascents of the soul. We should resist the reductive tendency to portray Socrates and Plato as the twin founts of Western technological rationalism; we should instead take seriously the more "spiritual" or "mystical" themes in Plato's work, themes that direct his readers toward something beyond that which is accessible to the everyday operations of thought.

Upon the death of Plato's nephew Speusippus, Xenocrates took over as scholarch of the Academy. Xenocrates had studied with Plato for perhaps as many as twenty years and was close enough to the master to accompany him to Sicily. According to reports recorded by Diogenes Laertius, Xenocrates "practiced an internal care and devoted an hour every day to silence" (ἑαυτῷ ἐμελέτα καὶ ὥραν μίαν…ἀπένεμε σιωπῇ, 4.11). Is this an indication that Xenocrates practiced some form of spiritual exercise? Like Speusippus before him, Xenocrates considered freedom from disturbance the ideal life; so it may be that his dedication to solitary silence was only a means of producing an interval of calm. Yet the expression "ἑαυτῷ ἐμελέτα" is pregnant. It suggests more than just keeping quiet; it suggests the practice of contemplation as purification. There is evidence that Xenocrates incorporated Pythagorean principles into his daily life, including vegetarianism, which the ancients associated with the doctrine of reincarnation and the purity of the soul. Such Pythagorean themes are at the heart of Plato's *Phaedo*, the *locus classicus* of the Platonic account of purification as preparation for the contemplation of, and identification with, ultimate reality. Xenocrates' abstention from meat was of interest to Porphyry, for whom the practice was integral to a life of purification leading to unification.

Porphyry's teacher, Plotinus, employs throughout his *Enneads* images that appear to derive from meditation techniques or spiritual exercises. He stresses repeatedly that the approach to the

PURIFICATION

One involves an inward turning of the soul and a shutting out of all externals. He advises the aspirant to unification to withdraw into himself, to forget all that is external and focus solely on That which is at once the Source and the Goal of all contemplation. The vision comes only to him who has prepared his soul to receive it. To prepare properly one must, as Plotinus puts it, "remove everything" (ἄφελε πάντα, 5.3.17). This is not an exclusively intellectual exercise; it certainly involves more than a daily regimen of regulated rites or behaviors. It is an act of something deeper—which at the same time is also something higher—than our intellect or the source of our external behaviors. It is an act of soul, of spirit, of that in us which is the source (ἡ ἀρχή) of our character and our mind. We are individual material beings only superficially; by "removing everything" we see through material individuality to a deeper metaphysical unity, to that in us which is always already one with the One.

Having completed his philosophical education in Alexandria, Plotinus joined the emperor Gordian's Persian expedition, hoping to make contact with and to study Eastern philosophy. Though Gordian's assassination put an end to this venture, we may presume that Plotinus already possessed an account of the wisdom that emanated from the East, for this provides the most plausible explanation of his desire to communicate with the sages who lived there. He longed to visit India, for example, to speak with men whose insights into reality coincided with his own. Plotinus' ontology, generally considered, is strikingly similar to the ontology presented in the *Bhagavad Gita*. Yet nowhere in Plotinus—nowhere in the whole of the ancient Greek philosophical tradition—do we find suggestions for meditative techniques as specific as those in the *Gita*'s sixth book. We must not suppose, however, that the Greek philosophers thought nothing of the relation between the practice of contemplation and one's circumstances and surroundings. The example of Xenocrates settles at least this much.

Purification, and thus contemplation as purification, involves exercising control over one's mind and body. According to Krishna's instructions in the *Gita*, one must sit in quiet isolation with the body still and firm, comfortable but under control, external physical reality forgotten, focusing one's mind only on the One, for this—unification with this—is one's goal. Krishna's words make clear that the practice of spiritual purification must combine intellectual and physical discipline: soul and body must work together, though of course with soul directing the relationship. Soul is the master, body the disciple. All spiritual exercises contribute in some way to reinforcing this hierarchy.

7

Whenever you want to indulge, recall that you prefer to ascend.

8

In sum: Does God exist? Before addressing this question we must specify some meaning for the word "God." By "God" we mean ὁ θεός, by which we mean the transcendent source of material reality, the unified wellspring of being, the principle and sustainer of this and every possible universe. We mean, in short, that which the Platonic tradition variously names the Good beyond being, the Source, the All-Pure, the One. How do we determine whether any such "being" exists? Certainly not through the methods and techniques of modern science; the testimony of our senses cannot help us. The question of God is a metaphysical question, the answer to which can be found only by and through the activity of logos. It is a question for our mind, or rather for our soul. But to have said this much is only to have made a beginning. It is not enough to refer the matter to soul, for we must consider the soul's condition, its soundness or unsoundness—its health. A soul burdened by the assumptions of materialism and empiricism will never ascend to truth, will never behold the divine. Such a soul is bound to the prison house of the body, unable to believe in anything more subtle than the matter under whose weight it labors.

The Platonic philosopher strives for something more; he ascends to truth by separating his soul from his body, which expression we should understand to designate, borrowing a formulation from the *Republic*, a release from the bonds and a turning away from the shadows of material reality (λύσις τε ἀπὸ τῶν δεσμῶν καὶ μεταστροφὴ ἀπὸ τῶν σκιῶν, *Republic* 532B6–7). At a minimum this entails being skeptical of the reductivist assumptions of modern philosophy. It may also involve a sustained and intentional effort to follow the road to metaphysical insight mapped out by the best of the Platonic philosophers. The charts and directions devised by these metaphysical cartographers are more than successive points on a grid determined by horizon or compass. The goal of our journey is not in question; we want to know *how* to proceed. The ancient Platonists long ago resolved this problem with one word: Purification.

As we have seen, purification is at once a physical, ethical, intellectual, and spiritual process. We must also understand that purification takes time; it is a long-term undertaking, a practice that requires concentrated effort and determined commitment throughout our lives. According to Porphyry's biography, Plotinus encountered the divine in his sixth decade; Porphyry himself experienced unification at the age of sixty-eight. For those who seek the truth purification is necessary; for no one is it quick or easy.

The very practice of purification is a challenge, a test, an ordeal. Everything we have written implies at least this much. But we have not written all there is to write, which implies something altogether different. We lack a thorough understanding of purification; we do not adequately comprehend its goal. We have had much to say, but no more than can be found in, inferred from, and elaborated by brooding over the ancient sources. Unfortunately, the "modern deviation" segregates us from these sources so profoundly that not only is there much that we do not know, presumably there is much that we do not know that we do not know. As a result, we can never simply practice purification; we must always also question the process, endeavor to deepen our understanding of its structure and meaning. In short, reflection upon purification is essential to the purificatory act. This is certainly true for us moderns; perhaps it has always been thus.

9

Concerning the man who commits himself to purification through contemplation, Arjuna's questions to Krishna must be our questions: How does he speak? How does he sit? How does he move?

EPILOGOS

It is better to be happy than to be unhappy. This may be a "truism," but it is false. It is at least incomplete. It is better that the bad man be *un*happy—better for himself and for everyone else. Only discontent will motivate him to change. He must *feel* miserable before he will believe that he *is* miserable. Having come to this realization, he will perhaps learn that misery is the inevitable effect of his vice. Only then will he desire to be good.

For the virtuous man, happiness is good indeed. But this is just to say that eudaimonia is good—good without qualification. This *is* a truism, despite the fact that we moderns no longer believe it or even understand what it means. This is the problem with modernity: under its influence one denies the truth, as one shuns goodness and disdains beauty. Unfortunately for us, modernity and eudaimonia may very well be incompatible.

Modernity *certainly* is incompatible with the one condition that is superior even to eudaimonia, namely unification with the divine—ὁμοίωσις θεῷ, τὸ ἑνωθῆναι, *henôsis, theôsis*. As sincerely as we want eudaimonia—and we *do* want it, for it is good—as diligent as we are in pursuit of this goal, we aim even more intently at a higher good, a further goal. We seek the divine, to know it and to be (with) it.

The progression from happiness to eudaimonia to unification is an ascent. It is a Platonic ascent out of the cave of obscure materiality into the light of intelligible truth. The source of illumination is the Source of the All. Some call it god; others call it God. We have called it the One. The name does not matter. What matters is the Thing Itself; also the ascent and the process through which one ascends—purification.

PURE: Modernity, Philosophy, and the One

The form of the book you have now completed mirrors the ascent; its content is meant to be pure, and to facilitate purification. As for the whole: it is nothing new; it is not original. It merely reformulates ideas that Platonists have espoused for millennia. If it does anything, it provides for a new generation of moderns a way up, which is also a way back, a way *out*.